Teach Yourself VISUALLY™

Windows® XP, Second Edition

Visual

by Paul McFedries

WILEY

Wiley Publishing, Inc.

Teach Yourself VISUALLY™ Windows® XP, Second Edition

Published by
Wiley Publishing, Inc.
111 River Street
Hoboken, NJ 07030-5774

Published simultaneously in Canada

Library of Congress Control Number: 2005921457

ISBN: 0-7645-7927-4

Manufactured in the United States of America

10 9 8 7 6 5 4 3

Trademark Acknowledgments

Contact Us

For general information on our other products and services please contact our Customer Care Department within the U.S. at 800-762-2974, outside the U.S. at 317-572-3993 or fax 317-572-4002.

For technical support please visit www.wiley.com/techsupport.

Wiley Publishing, Inc.

U.S. Sales

Contact Wiley at (800) 762-2974 or fax (317) 572-4002.

Praise for Visual Books

"Like a lot of other people, I understand things best when I see them visually. Your books really make learning easy and life more fun."

John T. Frey (Cadillac, MI)

"I have quite a few of your Visual books and have been very pleased with all of them. I love the way the lessons are presented!"

Mary Jane Newman (Yorba Linda, CA)

"I just purchased my third Visual book (my first two are dog-eared now!), and, once again, your product has surpassed my expectations.

Tracey Moore (Memphis, TN)

"I am an avid fan of your Visual books. If I need to learn anything, I just buy one of your books and learn the topic it in no time. Wonders! I have even trained my friends to give me Visual books as gifts."

Illona Bergstrom (Aventura, FL)

"Thank you for making it so clear. I appreciate it. I will buy many more Visual books."

J.P. Sangdong (North York, Ontario, Canada)

"I have several books from the Visual series and have always found them to be valuable resources."

Stephen P. Miller (Ballston Spa, NY)

"Thank you for the wonderful books you produce. It wasn't until I was an adult that I discovered how I learn – visually. Nothing compares to Visual books. I love the simple layout. I can just grab a book and use it at my computer, lesson by lesson. And I understand the material! You really know the way I think and learn. Thanks so much!"

Stacey Han (Avondale, AZ)

"I absolutely admire your company's work. Your books are terrific. The format is perfect, especially for visual learners like me. Keep them coming!"

Frederick A. Taylor, Jr. (New Port Richey, FL)

"I have several of your Visual books and they are the best I have ever used."

Stanley Clark (Crawfordville, FL)

"I bought my first Teach Yourself VISUALLY book last month. Wow. Now I want to learn everything in this easy format!"

Tom Vial (New York, NY)

"Thank you, thank you, thank you...for making it so easy for me to break into this high-tech world. I now own four of your books. I recommend them to anyone who is a beginner like myself."

Gay O'Donnell (Calgary, Alberta, Canada)

"I write to extend my thanks and appreciation for your books. They are clear, easy to follow, and straight to the point. Keep up the good work! I bought several of your books and they are just right! No regrets! I will always buy your books because they are the best."

Seward Kollie (Dakar, Senegal)

"Compliments to the chef!! Your books are extraordinary! Or, simply put, extra-ordinary, meaning way above the rest! THANKYOU THANKYOU THANKYOU! I buy them for friends, family, and colleagues."

Christine J. Manfrin (Castle Rock, CO)

"What fantastic teaching books you have produced! Congratulations to you and your staff. You deserve the Nobel Prize in Education in the Software category. Thanks for helping me understand computers."

Bruno Tonon (Melbourne, Australia)

"Over time, I have bought a number of your 'Read Less - Learn More' books. For me, they are THE way to learn anything easily. I learn easiest using your method of teaching."

José A. Mazón (Cuba, NY)

"I am an avid purchaser and reader of the Visual series, and they are the greatest computer books I've seen. The Visual books are perfect for people like myself who enjoy the computer, but want to know how to use it more efficiently. Your books have definitely given me a greater understanding of my computer, and have taught me to use it more effectively. Thank you very much for the hard work, effort, and dedication that you put into this series."

Alex Diaz (Las Vegas, NV)

Credits

Project Editor
Cricket Krengel

Acquisitions Editor
Jody Lefevere

Product Development Manager
Lindsay Sandman

Copy Editor
Scott Tullis

Technical Editor
Lee Musick

Editorial Manager
Robyn Siesky

Manufacturing
Allan Conley
Linda Cook
Paul Gilchrist
Jennifer Guynn

Proofreader
Vicki Broyles

Quality Control
Charles Spencer
Susan Moritz

Indexer
Johnna VanHoose

Book Design
Kathie Rickard

Production Coordinator
Maridee Ennis

Layout
Jennifer Heleine

Screen Artists
Jill Proll
Ronda David-Burroughs

Illustrators
Steven Amory
Matt Bell
Cheryl Grubbs
Sean Johanessen
Jake Mansfield
Rita Marley
Tyler Roloff
Diane Staver

Vice President and Executive Group Publisher
Richard Swadley

Vice President and Publisher
Barry Pruett

Composition Director
Debbie Stailey

About the Author

Paul McFedries is the president of Logophilia Limited, a technical writing company. While now primarily a writer, Paul has worked as a programmer, consultant, and Web site developer. Paul has written over 40 books that have sold over three million copies worldwide. These books include the Wiley title *Windows XP: Top 100 Simplified Tips & Tricks, Second Edition*.

Author's Acknowledgments

The book you hold in your hands is not only an excellent learning tool, but it is truly beautiful, as well. I am happy to have supplied the text that you will read, but the gorgeous images come from Wiley's crack team of artists and illustrators. The layout of the tasks, the accuracy of the spelling and grammar, and the veracity of the information are all the result of hard work performed by project editor Cricket Krengel, copy editor Scott Tullis, and technical editor Lee Musick. Thanks to all of you for your excellent work. My thanks, as well, to acquisitions editor Jody Lefevere for bringing me onboard, and to publisher Barry Pruett for recommending me.

TABLE OF CONTENTS

chapter 3 Creating and Editing Documents

chapter 4 Creating and Working with Images

TABLE OF CONTENTS

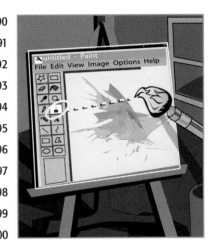

chapter 5

Playing Music and Other Media

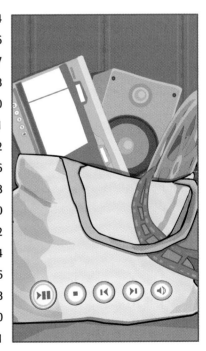

chapter 6

Working with Files

chapter 7

Sharing Your Computer with Others

TABLE OF CONTENTS

chapter **10**

Surfing the World Wide Web

chapter **11**

Sending and Receiving E-mail

TABLE OF CONTENTS

chapter 12 — Customizing Windows XP

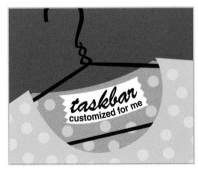

chapter 13

Maintaining Windows XP

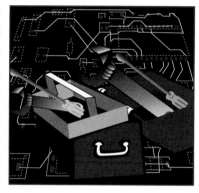

chapter 14

Networking with Windows XP

HOW TO USE THIS BOOK

Do you look at the pictures in a book or newspaper before anything else on a page? Would you rather see an image instead of read about how to do something? Search no further. This book is for you. Opening *Teach Yourself VISUALLY Windows XP* allows you to read less and learn more about the Windows XP program.

Who Needs This Book

This book is for a reader who has never used this particular technology or software application. It is also for more computer literate individuals who want to expand their knowledge of the different features that Windows XP has to offer.

Book Organization

Teach Yourself VISUALLY Windows XP has 14 chapters each of which teaches you a specific Windows XP topic. If you have never used Windows XP before, the first three chapters give you the basic techniques you require to get started. From there, each chapter is self-contained so that you can learn just the information you need at your own pace.

Chapter Organization

This book consists of sections, all listed in the book's table of contents. A *section* is a set of steps that show you how to complete a specific computer task.

Each section, usually contained on two facing pages, has an introduction to the task at hand, a set of full-color screen shots and steps that walk you through the task, and at least one tip. This format allows you to quickly look at a topic of interest and learn it instantly.

Chapters group together three or more sections with a common theme. A chapter may also contain pages that give you the background information needed to understand the sections in a chapter.

Chapter 1, "Getting Started with Windows XP" — This chapter gives you the basics of starting and stopping Windows XP, understanding the XP screen, and using a mouse.

Chapter 2, "Launching and Working with Programs" — This chapter shows you how to install and start programs, how to use menus, toolbars, and dialog boxes, and how to switch between program windows.

Chapter 3, "Creating and Editing Documents" — In this chapter, you learn how to create and open documents, edit document text, and save and print your work.

Chapter 4, "Creating and Working with Images" — This chapter shows you how to work with images in Windows XP, load images from the digital camera or scanner, and how to create your own images.

Chapter 5, "Playing Music and Other Media" — In this chapter you learn how to use Windows Media Player to play music, sound, and video files, audio CDs, and DVDs.

Chapter 6, "Working with Files" — This chapter shows you how to view, select, copy, and move files, burn files to a recordable CD, rename and delete files, and search for files.

Chapter 7, "Sharing Your Computer with Others" — This chapter shows you how to use Windows XP's User Accounts feature to enable multiple people to share a single computer.

Chapter 8, "Using Windows XP's Notebook Features" — In this chapter you learn how to use Windows XP's notebook computer features.

Chapter 9, "Getting Connected to the Internet" — This chapter shows you how to configure Windows XP to connect to the Internet.

Chapter 10, "Surfing the World Wide Web" — In this chapter you learn how to use the Internet Explorer program to browse the World Wide Web.

Chapter 11, "Sending and Receiving E-mail" — In this chapter you learn how to use the Outlook Express program to send and receive e-mail messages.

Chapter 12, "Customizing Windows XP" — This chapter shows you various ways to customize Windows XP to suit the way you work.

Chapter 13, "Maintaining Windows XP" — In this chapter you learn about some programs that enable you to perform routine maintenance that will keep your system running smoothly.

Chapter 14, "Networking with Windows XP" — This chapter shows you how to use Windows XP's networking features.

Who This Book is For

This book is highly recommended for the visual learner who wants to learn the basics of Windows XP, and who may or may not have prior experience with a computer.

What You Need to Use This Book

To perform the tasks in this book, you need a computer installed with Windows XP and one of the following:

- Recordable CD drive
- DVD drive
- Digital camera
- Image scanner

To get the most out of this book, you need to be running Windows XP with Service Pack 2 installed. However, most of the tasks work as written using the original Windows XP or Windows XP with Service Pack 1.

Using the Mouse

This book uses the following conventions to describe the actions you perform when using the mouse:

Click

Press your left mouse button once. You generally click your mouse to select something on the screen.

Double-click

Press your left mouse button twice. Double-clicking something on the computer screen generally opens whatever item you have double-clicked.

Right-click

Press your right mouse button. When you right-click anything on the computer screen, the program displays a shortcut menu containing commands specific to the selected item.

Click and Drag, and Release the Mouse

Move your mouse pointer and hover it over an item on the screen. Press and hold down the left mouse button. Now, move the mouse to where you want to place the item and then release the button. You use this method to move an item from one area of the computer screen to another.

The Conventions in This Book

A number of typographic and layout styles have been used throughout Teach Yourself Visually Windows XP to distinguish different types of information.

Bold

Bold type represents the names of commands and options that you interact with. Bold type also indicates text and numbers that you must type into a dialog box or window.

Italics

Italic words introduce a new term and are followed by a definition.

Numbered Steps

You must perform the instructions in numbered steps in order to successfully complete a section and achieve the final results.

Bulleted Steps

These steps point out various optional features. You do not have to perform these steps; they simply give additional information about a feature.

Indented Text

Indented text tells you what the program does in response to you following a numbered step. For example, if you click a certain menu command, a dialog box may appear, or a window may open. Indented text may also tell you what the final result is when you follow a set of numbered steps.

Notes

Notes give additional information. They may describe special conditions that may occur during an operation. They may warn you of a situation that you want to avoid, for example the loss of data. A note may also cross reference a related area of the book. A cross reference may guide you to another chapter, or another section with the current chapter.

Icons and buttons

Icons and buttons are graphical representations within the text. They show you exactly what you need to click to perform a step.

 You can easily identify the tip in any section by looking for the TIP icon. Tips offer additional information, including tips, hints, and tricks. You can use the TIP information to go beyond what you have learned in the steps.

CHAPTER 1

Getting Started with Windows XP

Are you ready to learn about Windows XP? In this chapter, you learn the basics of starting and activating Windows XP, getting help, and shutting down your system.

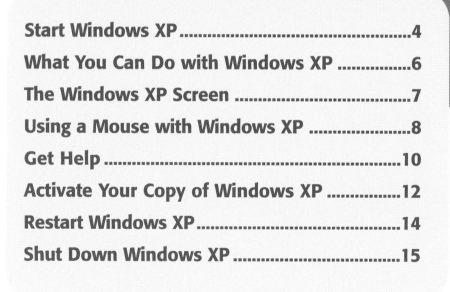

Start
Windows XP

When you turn on your computer, Windows XP starts automatically, but you may have to navigate a screen or dialog box along the way.

How you start Windows XP depends on whether you are running Windows XP Home or Windows XP Professional. Note, too, that the first time you start your computer, you may need to run through a series of configuration steps.

Start Windows XP Home

START WINDOWS XP HOME

① Turn on your computer.

● The Welcome screen appears.

Note: If your version of Windows XP Home is configured with just a single user, then you will bypass the Welcome screen and go directly to the desktop.

② Click the icon that corresponds to your Windows XP user name.

Windows XP may ask you to enter your password.

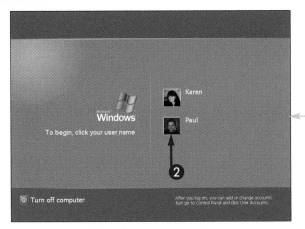

③ Type your password.

Note: The password characters appear as dots so that no one else can read your password.

④ Click 🔁.

The Windows XP desktop appears.

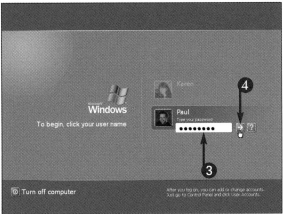

START WINDOWS XP PROFESSIONAL

1 Turn on your computer.

● The Welcome to Windows dialog box appears.

2 Press `Ctrl` + `Alt` + `Delete`.

The Log On to Windows dialog box appears.

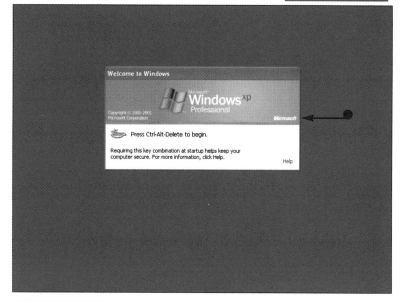

3 Type your user name.

4 Type your password.

Note: *The password characters appear as asterisks so that no one else can read your password.*

5 Click **OK.**

The Windows XP desktop appears.

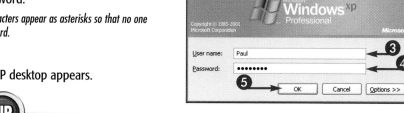

What happens if I forget my Windows XP Home password?

Most Windows XP Home user accounts that are password protected are also set up with a password "hint" — usually a word or phrase designed to jog your memory. You choose the question when you set your password, as explained in the section titled "Protect an Account with a Password" in Chapter 7. If you forget your password, click ? to see the password hint.

What You Can Do with Windows XP

Windows XP is an operating system that contains a collection of tools, programs, and resources. Here is a sampling of what you can do with them.

Get Work Done

With Windows XP, you can run programs that enable you to get your work done more efficiently, such as a word processor for writing memos and letters, a spreadsheet for making calculations, and a database for storing information. Windows XP comes with some of these programs (such as the Word Pad program you learn about in Chapter 3), and there are others you can purchase and install separately.

Create and Edit Pictures

Windows XP comes with lots of features that let you work with images. You can create your own pictures from scratch, import images from a scanner or digital camera, or download images from the Internet. After you create or acquire an image, you can edit it, print it, or send it via e-mail. You learn about these and other picture tasks in Chapter 4.

Play Music and Other Media

Windows XP has treats for your ears as well as your eyes. You can listen to audio CDs, play digital sound and video clips, watch DVD movies, tune in to Internet radio stations, and copy audio files to a recordable CD. You learn about these multimedia tasks in Chapter 5.

Get on the Internet

Windows XP makes connecting to the Internet easy (see Chapter 9). And after you are on the Net, Windows XP has all the tools you need to get the most out of your experience. For example, you can use Internet Explorer to surf the World Wide Web (see Chapter 10) and Outlook Express to send and receive e-mail (see Chapter 11).

Before getting to the specifics of working with Windows XP, take a few seconds to familiarize yourself with the basic screen elements.

Desktop
This is the Windows XP "work area," meaning that it is where you work with your programs and documents.

Mouse Pointer
When you move your mouse, this pointer moves along with it.

Desktop Icon
An icon on the desktop represents a program or Windows XP feature. A program you install often adds its own icon on the desktop.

Time
This is the current time on your computer. To see the current date, position the mouse over the time. To change the date or time, double-click the time.

Notification Area
This area displays small icons that notify you about things that are happening on your computer. For example, you see notifications if your printer runs out of paper or if an update to Windows XP is available over the Internet.

Start Button
You use this button to start programs and launch many of Windows XP's features.

Taskbar
The programs you have open appear in the taskbar. You use this area to switch between programs if you have more than one running at a time.

Windows XP was built with the mouse in mind, so it pays to learn early the basic mouse techniques that you will use throughout your Windows career.

If you have never used a mouse before, there are two keys to learning how to use it: Keep all your movements slow and deliberate, and practice the techniques in this section as much as you can.

Using a Mouse with Windows XP

CLICK THE MOUSE

① Position the mouse ⌖ over the object you want to work with.

② Click the left mouse button.

● Depending on the object, Windows XP either selects the object or performs some operation in response to the click (such as displaying the Start menu).

DOUBLE-CLICK THE MOUSE

① Move the mouse ⌖ over the object you want to work with.

② Click the left mouse button twice in quick succession.

● Windows XP usually performs some operation in response to the double-click action (such as displaying the Date and Time Properties dialog box).

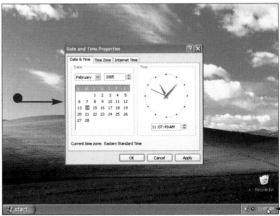

RIGHT-CLICK THE MOUSE

1 Position the mouse ↖ over the object you want to work with.

2 Click the right mouse button.

● Windows XP displays a shortcut menu when you right-click something.

Note: *The contents of the shortcut menu depend on the object you right-clicked.*

CLICK AND DRAG THE MOUSE

1 Position the mouse ↖ over the object you want to work with.

2 Hold down the left mouse button.

3 Move the mouse to drag the selected object.

● In most cases, the object moves along with the mouse ↖.

4 Release the mouse button when the selected object is repositioned.

TIPS

Why does Windows XP sometimes not recognize my double-clicks?

Try to double-click as quickly as you can, and be sure not to move the mouse between clicks. If you continue to have trouble, click **start, Control Panel, Printers and Other Hardware,** and then **Mouse**. In the Double-click speed group, click and drag the slider to the left (toward Slow).

How can I set up my mouse for a left-hander?

Click **start, Control Panel, Printers and Other Hardware**, and then **Mouse**. Click **Switch primary and secondary buttons** (☐ changes to ☑).

Get Help

You can find out more about Windows XP, learn how to perform a task, or troubleshoot problems by accessing the Help system.

Most of the Help system is arranged into various topics, such as "Customizing your computer" and "Fixing a problem." Each topic offers a number of subtopics, and each subtopic contains a collection of related tasks, articles, tutorials, and other items.

Get Help

1 Click **start**.

The Start menu appears.

2 Click **Help and Support**.

The Help and Support Center window appears.

3 Click a topic.

A list of subtopics appears for the topic you selected.

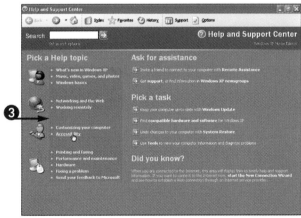

④ Click a subtopic.

● A list of Help articles appears for the subtopic you select.

⑤ Click an article, task, overview, or tutorial.

● The item you select appears in the Help and Support Center window.

⑥ Read the article.

Note: To return to a previous Help and Support Center screen, click **Back** until you get to the screen you want.

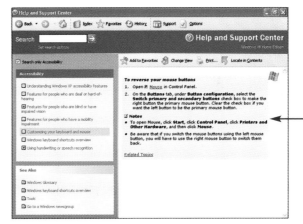

How do I get help for a specific program?
Almost all Windows programs have their own Help features. You can access Help in a specific program in three main ways:

● Click **Help** from the menu, and then click the command that runs the Help features (it may be called **Help Contents**, **Help Topics**, or **Program Help**, where *Program* is the name of the program (for example, **Microsoft Word Help**).

● Press F1.

● In a dialog box, click ?, and then click a control to see a description of the control.

Activate Your Copy of Windows XP

To avoid piracy, Microsoft requires that each copy of Windows XP be activated. Otherwise, your copy of Windows XP will refuse to run after about 60 days.

Activate Your Copy of Windows XP

① Click **start**.

The Start menu appears.

② Click **All Programs**.

③ Click **Activate Windows**.

The Activate Windows screen appears.

Note: If you see an icon in the taskbar's notification area that looks like a set of keys (🔑), you can click that icon to go directly to the Activate Windows screen.

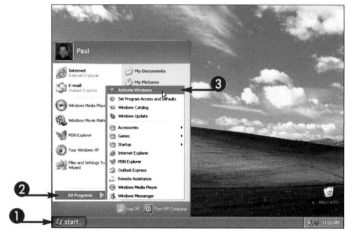

④ Click the radio button choice for Internet activation (○ changes to ◉).

⑤ Click **Next**.

Note: If you do not have Internet access, click the radio button choice for telephone activation, instead.

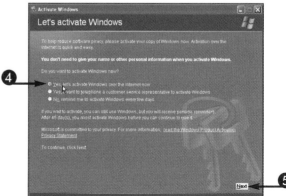

The Register with Microsoft? window appears.

Note: Registering with Microsoft is optional; you can still activate your copy of Windows XP without registering.

6 Click **No, I don't want to register now; let's just activate Windows** (○ changes to ◉).

7 Click **Next**.

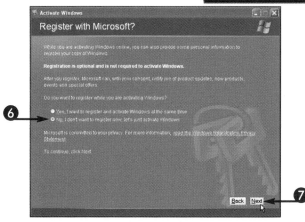

Windows XP confirms that it has been activated.

8 Click **OK**.

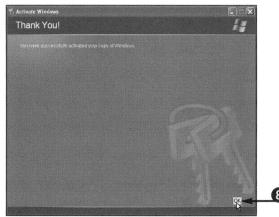

TIPS

Can I activate Windows XP on more than one computer?

No, not usually. The activation process creates a special value that is unique to your computer's hardware configuration. When you activate Windows XP, your copy of the program is associated with this unique hardware value, which means your copy will only ever work with that one computer. However, if that computer breaks down, you can telephone Microsoft to let them know and they should allow you to activate XP on another computer.

I do not see the Activate Windows command on my All Programs menu. Why not?

This probably means that your copy of Windows XP has already been activated. If your computer came with Windows XP preinstalled, the manufacturer may have taken care of the activation process for you. To confirm this, click **start, All Programs, Accessories, System Tools,** and then **Activate Windows**. The Activate Windows screen appears and tells you your activation status.

You can restart Windows XP, which means it shuts down and starts up again immediately. This is useful if your computer is running slow or acting funny. Sometimes a restart solves the problem.

Knowing how to restart Windows XP also comes in handy when you install a program or device that requires a restart to function properly. If you are busy right now, you can always opt to restart your computer yourself later on when it is more convenient.

Restart Windows XP

1 Shut down all your running programs.

Note: Be sure to save your work as you close your programs.

2 Click **start**.

3 Click **Turn Off Computer**.

The Turn off computer window appears.

Note: In Windows XP Professional, the Shut Down Windows dialog box appears.

4 Click **Restart**.

*Note: In Windows XP Professional, click [⌄] , click **Restart**, and then click **OK**.*

Windows XP shuts down and your computer restarts.

When you complete your work for the day, you should shut down Windows XP. However, do not just shut off your computer's power. Follow the proper steps to avoid damaging files on your system.

Shutting off the computer's power without properly exiting Windows XP can cause two problems. First, if you have unsaved changes in some open documents, you will lose those changes. Second, you could damage one or more Windows XP system files, which could make your system unstable.

Shut Down Windows XP

① Shut down all your running programs.

Note: Be sure to save your work as you close your programs.

② Click **start**.

③ Click **Turn Off Computer**.

The Turn off computer window appears.

Note: In Windows XP Professional, the Shut Down Windows dialog box appears.

④ Click **Turn Off**.

*Note: In Windows XP Professional, click ▼, click **Shut down**, and then click **OK**.*

Windows XP shuts down and turns off your computer.

Launching and Working with Programs

On its own, Windows XP does not do very much. To do something useful with your computer, you need to work with a program, either one that comes with Windows XP or one that you install yourself. In this chapter, you learn how to install, launch, and work with programs.

Install a Program

If Windows XP does not come with a program that you need, you can purchase the program yourself and then install it on your computer.

How you start the installation process depends on whether the program comes on a CD, DVD, floppy disk, or from the Internet.

Install a Program

INSTALL FROM A CD OR DVD

① Insert the program's CD or DVD into the appropriate disk drive.

● The software's installation program begins.

Note: If a program on CD or DVD does not launch its installation program automatically after you insert the disc, see the instructions in the "Install from a Floppy Disk" section of this task.

② Follow the installation instructions provided by the program.

Note: Installation steps vary from program to program.

INSTALL FROM A FILE DOWNLOADED FROM THE INTERNET

① Use My Computer to find the downloaded file.

Note: To view a file with My Computer, see the task "View Your Files" in Chapter 6.

② Double-click the file.

The software's installation program begins.

Note: For compressed files, extract the files, and then double-click the Setup file. See the "Extract Files from a Compressed Folder" task in Chapter 6.

③ Follow the installation instructions provided by the program.

INSTALL FROM A FLOPPY DISK

1 If your CD-based program does not install automatically, insert the floppy disk or the CD.

Note: If your program comes on multiple floppy disks, insert the disk labeled "Disk 1," "Setup," or something similar.

2 Click **start**.

3 Click **Control Panel**.

The Control Panel window appears.

4 Click **Add or Remove Programs**.

The Add or Remove Programs window appears.

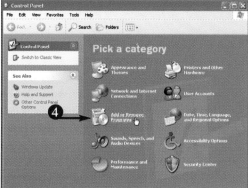

TIP

How do I find my software's product key or serial number?

The product key or serial number is crucial because many programs will not install until you enter the number. Look for a sticker attached to the back or inside of the CD case. Also look on the registration card, the CD itself, or the back of the box. If you downloaded the program, the number should appear on the download screen and on the e-mail receipt that is sent to you.

00123 45600

continued

You can use the Add New Programs feature to install any program on your computer. However, you really only need it for those rare programs (such as those on floppy disks) that do not launch their installation programs automatically.

Install a Program *(continued)*

5 Click **Add New Programs**.

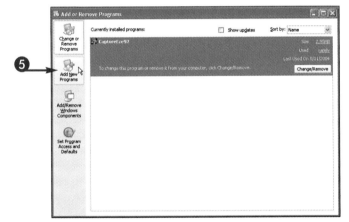

6 Click **CD or Floppy**.

The Install Program From Floppy Disk or CD-ROM dialog box appears.

⑦ Click **Next**.

Windows XP looks for the installation program on the floppy disk or CD.

Note: *If Windows XP cannot find the program, click **Browse**, use the Browse dialog box to search for and click the program, and then click **Open**.*

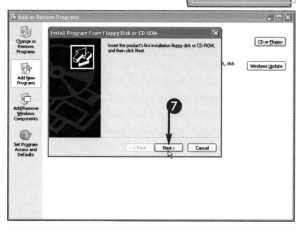

⑧ Click **Finish**.

The software's installation program begins.

⑨ Follow the installation instructions provided by the program.

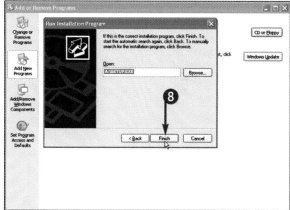

TIP

What is the difference between a "typical" and "custom" installation?

A "typical" installation automatically installs only those program components that people use most often. In a "custom" installation, you select which components are installed, where they are installed, and so on. The custom option is best suited for experienced users, so you are usually better off choosing the typical install.

Start a Program

To work with any program, you must first tell Windows XP which program you want to run. Windows XP then launches the program and displays it on the desktop.

① Click **start**.

The Start menu appears.

② Click **All Programs**.

The All Programs menu appears.

Note: If the program you want to launch appears on the Start menu, click the program and skip the rest of the steps in this section.

③ Click the submenu that contains your program.

④ Click the icon for the program you want to launch.

● The program appears on the desktop.

● Windows XP adds a button for the program to the taskbar.

You work with a program by manipulating the various features of its window.

Minimize Button

You click **Minimize** ( ) to remove the window from the desktop and display only the window's taskbar icon. The window is still open, but not active.

System Menu Icon

Clicking this icon enables you to work with program windows via the keyboard.

Title Bar

The title bar displays the name of the program. In some programs, the title bar also displays the name of the open document. You can also use the title bar to move the window.

Menu Bar

The menu bar contains the pull-down menus for Windows XP and most Windows XP software.

Maximize Button

To enlarge the window either from the taskbar or so that it takes up the entire desktop, click **Maximize** ( ).

Close Button

When you click **Close** ( ), the program shuts down.

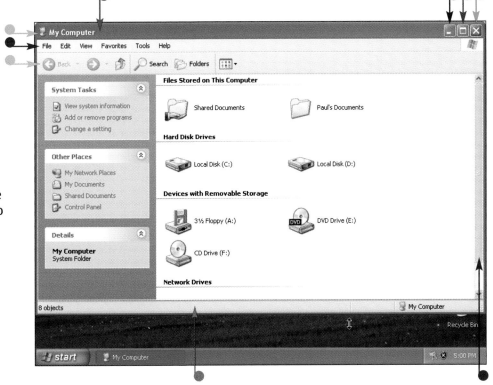

Toolbar

Buttons that offer easy access to common program commands and features are located in the toolbar. Some buttons are commands and some have lists from which you can make a choice.

Status Bar

The status bar displays information about the current status of the program.

Scrollbar

You use the scrollbar to navigate a document. You use a vertical scrollbar to navigate up and down in the document; you use a horizontal scrollbar to navigate left and right in a document.

Using Pull-Down Menus

When you are ready to work with a program, use the pull-down menus to access the program's commands and features.

The items in a pull-down menu are either commands that execute some action in the program, or features that you turn on and off.

Using Pull-Down Menus

RUN COMMANDS

① Click the name of the menu you want to display.

● The program displays the menu.

You can also display a menu by holding down the **Alt** key and pressing the underlined letter in the menu name.

② Click the command you want to run.

The program runs the command.

● If your command is in a submenu, click the submenu and then click the desired command.

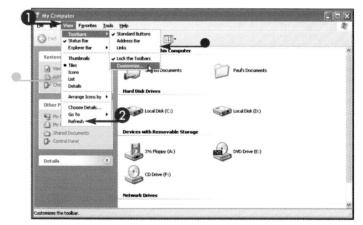

TURN FEATURES ON AND OFF

① Click the name of the menu you want to display.

● The program displays the menu.

② Click the menu item.

Click a submenu if your command is not on the Main menu.

● Toggle features are either turned on (indicated by ☑) or off (no check mark appears).

● Click an option feature to turn it on (indicated by ◉) and turn off the previously activated item.

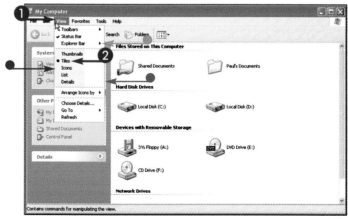

You can access commands faster using the toolbar. Most programs come with one or more toolbars, which are collections of buttons that in most cases give you one-click access to the program's most common features.

Using Toolbars

① Click the Toolbar button that represents the command or list.

Note: If the Toolbar button remains "pressed" after you click it, the button toggles a feature on and off and the feature is now on. To turn the feature off, click the button to "unpress" it.

● The program drops down the list or executes the command.

② Click the list item that represents the command.

The program runs the command.

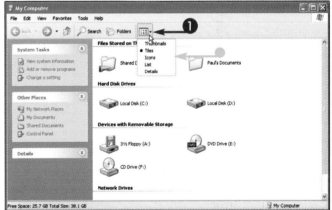

DISPLAY AND HIDE TOOLBARS

① Click **View**.

② Click **Toolbars**.

③ Click the name of the toolbar you want to display or hide.

● If the toolbar is currently displayed (indicated by ☑ in the Toolbars menu), the program hides the toolbar.

If the toolbar is currently hidden, the program displays the toolbar (indicated by ☑ in the Toolbars menu).

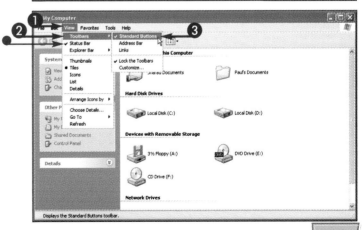

Dialog boxes appear when a program needs you to provide information. You provide that information by manipulating various types of controls.

Option Button
Clicking an option button turns on a program feature. Only one option button in a group can be turned on at a time. When you click an option button, it changes from ○ to ◉.

Tab
The various tabs in a dialog box display different sets of controls. You can choose from these settings in a dialog box to achieve a variety of results in Windows XP.

Check Box
Clicking a check box toggles a program feature on and off. If you are turning a feature on, the check box changes from ☐ to ☑; if you are turning the feature off, the check box changes from ☑ to ☐.

Combo Box
The combo box combines both a text box and a list box.

Drop-Down List Box
A drop-down list box displays only the selected item from a list. You can open the list to select a different item.

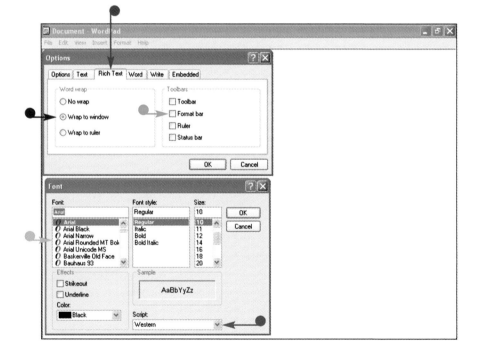

Spin Button
The spin button enables you to choose a numeric value.

Text Box
A text box enables you to enter typed text.

List Box
A list box displays a list of items from which you can select a relatively large number of choices. There are various types of lists, and you need to know how to use them all.

Command Button
Clicking a command button executes the command written on the button face. For example, you can click **OK** to put settings you choose in a dialog box into effect, or you can click **Cancel** to close the dialog box without changing the settings.

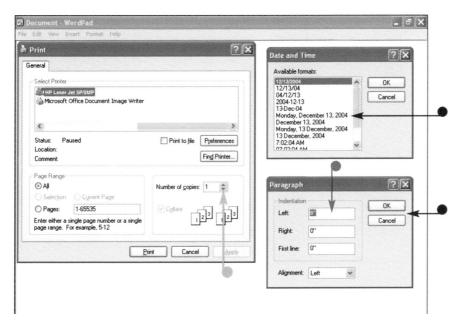

Using Dialog Boxes

You use dialog boxes to control how a program works. Dialog boxes appear frequently, so you need to know how to use them to get the most out of any program.

For example, when you print a document, you use the Print dialog box to specify the number of copies you want printed.

USING A TEXT BOX

1 Click inside the text box.

● A blinking, vertical bar (called a *cursor*) appears inside the text box.

2 Use the **Backspace** or **Delete** keys to delete any existing characters.

3 Type your text.

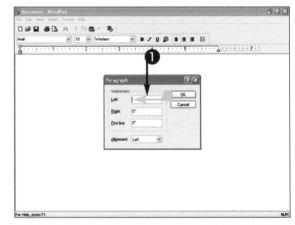

ENTER A VALUE WITH A SPIN BUTTON

1 Click the top arrow on 🔼 to increase the value.

2 Click the bottom arrow on 🔽 to decrease the value.

● You can also type the value in the text box.

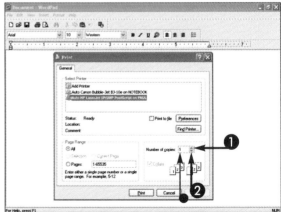

SELECT A LIST BOX ITEM

① If necessary, click ⊡ to scroll down the list and bring the item you want to select into view.

Note: See the section "Work with Program Windows" to learn how to use scrollbars.

② Click the item.

● Click ⊡ to scroll back up through the list.

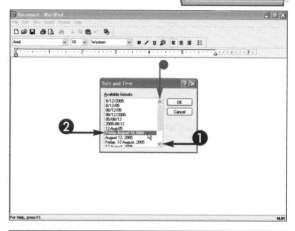

SELECT AN ITEM USING A COMBO BOX

● Type the item name in the text box, or click the item in the list box to select it.

SELECT AN ITEM FROM A DROP-DOWN LIST BOX

① Click ⊡.

● The list appears.

② Click the item in the list that you want to select.

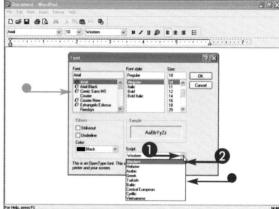

TIP

Are there keyboard shortcuts I can use to make dialog boxes easier to work with?

Yes. Here are the most useful shortcuts:

Enter	Selects the default command button (which is indicated with a highlight around it).
Esc	Cancels the dialog box (which is the same as clicking **Cancel**).
Alt +*letter*	Selects the control that has the *letter* underlined.
Tab	Moves forward through the dialog box controls.
Shift + **Tab**	Moves backward through the dialog box controls.
⬆ and ⬇	Move up and down within the current option button group.
Alt + ⬇	Drops down the selected combo box or drop-down list box.

Work with Program Windows

You need to know how to work with program windows so that you can keep your desktop neat and uncluttered.

For example, you can minimize a window to clear it from the desktop. Similarly, you can move or resize windows so that they do not overlap each other.

Work with Program Windows

MINIMIZE A WINDOW

1 Click ▬.

● The window disappears from the screen, but its taskbar button remains visible.

MAXIMIZE A WINDOW

1 Click  .

● The window enlarges to fill the entire desktop.

Note: You can also maximize a window by double-clicking its title bar.

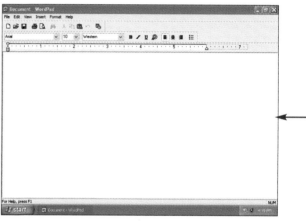

TIPS

Is there a faster way to minimize all my open windows?

The fastest way is to right-click the taskbar, and then click **Show the Desktop**. This command minimizes all your open windows at once.

Is it possible to maximize a minimized window?

To do this, right-click the window's taskbar button, and then click **Maximize**.

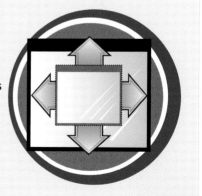

continued

Work with Program Windows *(continued)*

Are you ready for more window techniques? Windows XP uses many windows, so the more you know, the faster and more efficiently you can work.

For example, you should know how to *restore* **a window. This means that you return the window to its original size and location after you have either minimized it or maximized it.**

Work with Program Windows *(continued)*

RESTORE A WINDOW

1 If the window is maximized, click Restore ( ).

2 If the window is minimized, click its taskbar button.

● The window returns to its previous size and location.

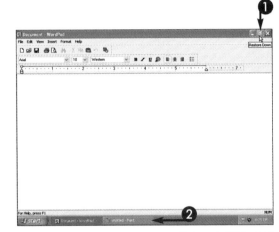

CLOSE A WINDOW

① Click .

The window disappears from the screen.

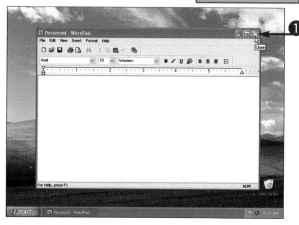

● If the window has a taskbar button, the button disappears from the taskbar.

Note: If the window contains a document, the program may ask if you want to save any changes you made in the document before closing. See the section "Shut Down a Program" to learn how to save before closing.

TIP

Can I work with program windows via the keyboard?

Yes, by using the system menu that comes with each window. Click the system menu icon in the upper-left corner to display the menu, press ⬆ and ⬇ on the keyboard to highlight the command you want, and then press Enter. If you choose Move or Size from the system menu, use the keyboard ⬆, ⬇, ⬅, and ➡ to move or size the window, and then press Enter.

continued

If your windows overlap each other, making it hard to read what is in other windows, you can move the windows around or resize them.

Work with Program Windows *(continued)*

CHANGE THE WINDOW SIZE

1 Position the mouse pointer (↖) over the window border that you want to move.

● The ↖ changes to a two-headed arrow (←→).

Note: *If the pointer does not change, it means the window cannot be resized.*

2 Click and drag the ←→ to make the window larger or smaller.

Windows XP moves the border along with the ←→ .

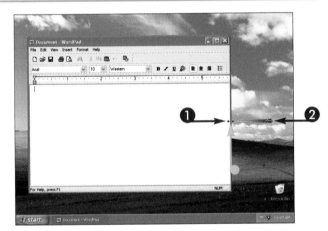

3 Release the mouse button.

● Windows XP resizes the window.

Note: *To resize two borders at once, click and drag any corner of the window.*

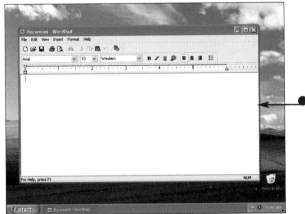

MOVE A WINDOW

1 Position the ▷ over an empty section of the window's title bar.

2 Click and drag the ▷ in the direction you want the window to move.

Windows XP moves the window along with the ▷.

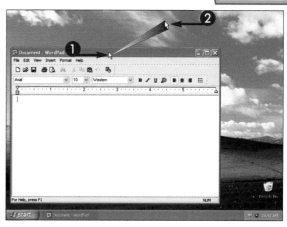

3 Release the mouse button.

● Windows XP moves the window.

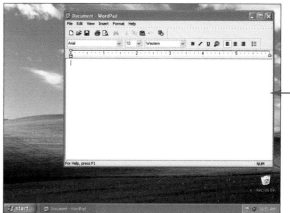

When I have several windows open, is there an easier way to size them so that none of the windows overlap?

Use Windows XP's *tiling* feature: Right-click an empty section of the taskbar and then click either **Tile Windows Vertically** or **Tile Windows Horizontally**. Windows XP divides the desktop to give each window an equal amount of space.

When I have several windows open, is there an easier way to move them so that the windows are arranged neatly?

Use Windows XP's *cascading* feature: Right-click an empty section of the taskbar and then click **Cascade Windows**. Windows XP arranges the windows in a tidy diagonal pattern from the top-left corner of the desktop.

Using Scrollbars

If the entire content of a document does not fit inside a window, you can see the rest of the document using the window's scrollbars to move vertically or horizontally.

Scrollbars also appear in many list boxes, so knowing how to work with scrollbars also helps you use dialog boxes.

Using Scrollbars

SCROLL UP OR DOWN IN A WINDOW

1 Click 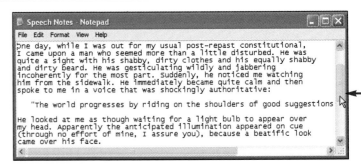 or ⌃ or click and drag the vertical scroll box down or up to scroll through a window.

● The text scrolls down or up.

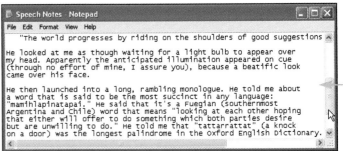

SCROLL RIGHT OR LEFT IN A WINDOW

① Click ▷ or ◁ or click and drag the horizontal scroll box.

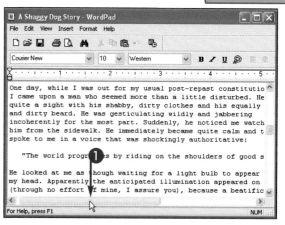

● The text scrolls right or left.

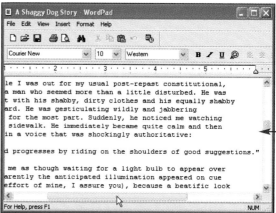

TIP

What is the wheel on my mouse used for?

Not everyone's mouse has a wheel, but if yours does, you can use the wheel for scrolling up or down in a document. It works the same way as clicking ▽ or △. Move the wheel backward, toward your arm, and the document scrolls down; move the wheel forward, toward your computer, and the document scrolls up.

Switch between Programs

With Windows XP, if you are *multitasking* — running two or more programs at once — you need to know how to switch from one program to another.

1 Click the taskbar button of the program to which you want to switch.

Note: *A program does not have to be minimized to the taskbar for you to use the program's taskbar button.*

● Windows XP brings the program's window to the foreground.

Note: *You can also switch to another window by clicking the window, even if it is the background.*

Note: *If you only have two programs open, you can switch between them from the keyboard by pressing* **Alt** + **Enter** .

Note: *If you have more than two windows open, hold down* **Alt** *and repeatedly press* **Tab** *until you get to the window in which you want to work.*

When you finish working with a program, you need to shut it down to avoid cluttering your desktop. This is different from simply closing a window because you may also have to save your work.

Closing unnecessary programs also saves resources, which makes Windows XP run faster.

Shut Down a Program

① Click ☒.

● If you have any unsaved changes, the program asks if you want to save your work.

② Click **Yes** to save your changes. If you do not want to save your changes, click **No**.

Note: If the document is new, saving it is a bit more complicated. See the section "Save a Document" in Chapter 3 for the details.

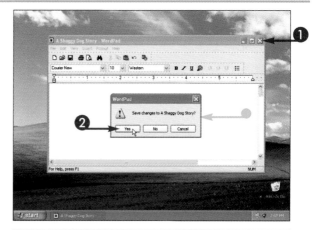

The window disappears from the screen.

● The program's taskbar button disappears from the taskbar.

Uninstall a Program

When you plan to no longer use a program, you should uninstall it from your computer.

Removing unused programs frees up disk space and makes your All Programs menu easier to navigate.

Uninstall a Program

① Click **start**.

② Click **Control Panel**.

The Control Panel window appears.

③ Click **Add or Remove Programs**.

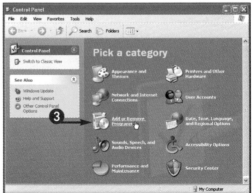

The Add or Remove Programs window appears.

④ Click **Remove** (or **Change/Remove**) for the program you want to uninstall.

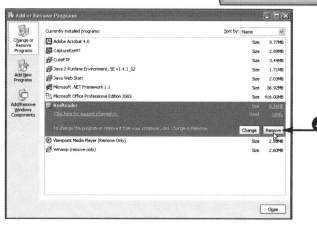

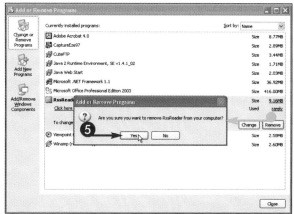

● The program asks you to confirm that you want to uninstall it.

⑤ Click **Yes**.

The program's uninstall procedure begins.

⑥ Follow the instructions on the screen, which vary from program to program.

 TIPS

Is there a quicker way to uninstall a program?

Many programs come with their own uninstall command. Click **start**, click **All Programs**, and then click the program name. If you see a command that includes the word *Uninstall*, click that command to begin the uninstall procedure.

What is the difference between an Automatic and a Custom uninstall?

Some programs give you a choice of uninstall procedures. The Automatic uninstall requires no input from you. It is the easiest, safest choice and therefore the one you should choose. The Custom uninstall gives you more control, but is more complex and only suitable for experienced users.

3

Creating and Editing Documents

To get productive with Windows XP, you need to know how to work with documents. In this chapter, you learn how to create, save, open, edit, and print documents.

Come to Our Open House!

On June 21, everyone is welcome to visit the State Museum for our Open House Day!

We will have several guest speakers, and will be opening our "Documents of American History" exhibit, in our newly renovated North Wing.

Admission is free!

Museum hours from
10 a.m. to 6 p.m.
We look forward to seeing you there!

Notepad

Understanding Documents

Documents are files that you create or edit yourself. The four examples shown here are the basic document types that you can create using the programs that come with Windows XP.

Text Document

A text document is one that includes only the characters that you see on your keyboard, plus a few others (see the section "Insert Special Symbols" in this chapter). A text document contains no special formatting, such as colored text or bold formatting, although you can change the font. In Windows XP you normally use the Notepad program to create text documents (although you can also use WordPad).

Word Processing Document

A word processing document contains text and other symbols, but you can format those characters to improve the look of the document. For example, you can change the size, color, and typeface, and you can make words bold or italic. In Windows XP, you use the WordPad program to create word processing — or Rich Text Format — documents.

Drawing

A drawing in this context is a digital image created using special "tools" that create lines, boxes, polygons, special effects, and free-form shapes. In Windows XP, you use the Paint program to create drawings. See the section "Create a Drawing" in Chapter 4.

E-mail Message

An e-mail message is a document that you send to another person via the Internet. Most e-mail messages use plain text, but some programs support formatted text, images, and other effects. In Windows XP, you use the Outlook Express program to create and send e-mail messages (see Chapter 11, "Sending and Receiving E-mail").

You can create a new document
to hold your work.

**Many Windows XP programs (such as
WordPad and Paint) create a new
document for you automatically when
you begin the program.**

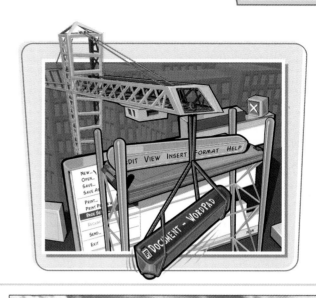

Create a Document

CREATE A DOCUMENT WITHIN A PROGRAM

1 Start the program you want to work with.

2 Click **File**.

3 Click **New**.

Note: Another way to create a document is to click New Document ( ).

Note: In most programs, you can also press Ctrl + N *to create a new
document.*

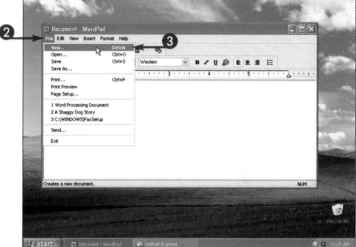

● If the program supports more than one type of file,
the program asks which type you want to create.

4 Click the document type you want.

5 Click **OK**.

The program creates the new document.

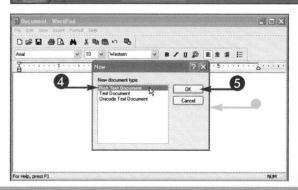

Save a Document

After you create a document and make any changes to it, you can save the document to preserve your work.

When you work on a document, Windows XP stores the changes in your computer's memory, which is erased each time you shut down your computer. Saving the document preserves your changes on your computer's hard drive.

1 Click **File**.

2 Click **Save**.

Note: In most programs, you can also press `Ctrl` *+* `S` *or click Save (* 🖫 *).*

Note: If you saved the document previously, your changes are now preserved. You do not need to follow the rest of the steps in this section.

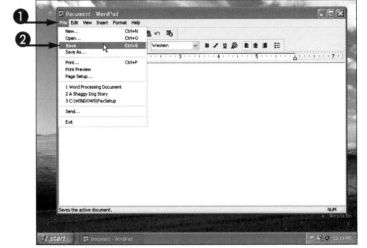

If this is a new document that you have never saved before, the Save As dialog box appears.

3 Click **My Documents**.

Note: If you want to save the document in some other folder, click the Down Arrow (⌄ *) in the **Save in** list, click the disk drive that contains the folder, and then double-click the name of the folder.*

● Windows XP opens the My Documents folder.

④ Click in the **File name** text box and type the name you want to use for the document.

*Note: The name you type can be up to 255 characters long, but it cannot include the following characters: < > , ? : " \ *.*

⑤ Click **Save**.

● The file name you typed appears in the program's title bar.

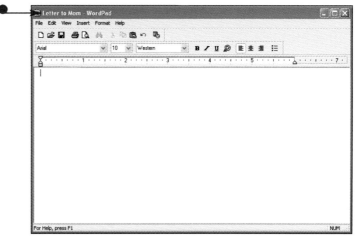

Can I create different types of documents in a program?

Yes, in some cases. With WordPad, for example, you can create both word processing documents and text documents. However, a program such as Notepad only supports text documents. If the program supports multiple document types, the Save As dialog box will have a drop-down list named **Save as type** (or something similar). Use that list to choose the document type you want.

Open a Document

To work with a document that you have saved in the past, you need to open the document in the program that you used to create it.

Open a Document

① Start the program you want to work with.

② Click **File**.

Note: If you see a list of the most recently opened documents near the bottom of the File menu, and you see the document you want, click the name to open it. You can skip the rest of the steps in this task.

③ Click **Open**.

Note: In most programs, you can also press **Ctrl** + **O** *or click Open ( ).*

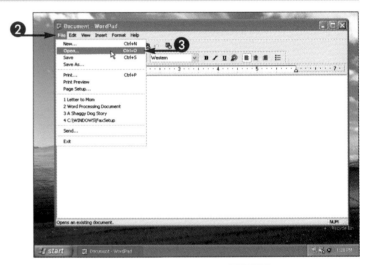

④ Click **My Documents**.

*Note: If you want to open the document from some other folder, click in the **Look in** list, click the disk drive that contains the folder, and then double-click the name of the folder.*

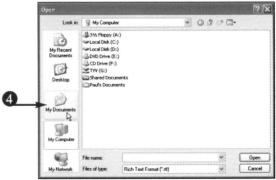

Windows XP opens the My Documents folder.

⑤ Click the document.

⑥ Click **Open**.

The document appears in the program window.

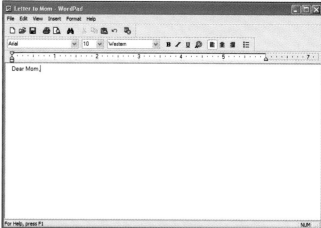

Is there a more direct way to open a document?

Yes there is. You do not always need to open the program first. Instead, open the folder that contains the document and then double-click the document. Windows XP automatically launches the programs and opens the document.

① Click **start**.

② Click **My Documents**.

The My Documents folder appears.

③ Double-click the document.

Windows XP starts the program in which you created the document and then opens the document.

Make a Copy of a Document

When you need to create a document that is nearly identical to an existing document, rather than creating the new document from scratch, you can save time by making a copy of the existing document, and then modifying the copy as needed.

① Start the program you want to work with.

② Click **File**.

③ Click **Save As**.

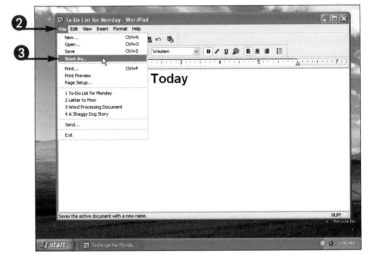

The Save As dialog box appears.

④ Click **My Documents**.

Note: *If you want to save the copy in some other folder, click* ☑ *in the* **Save in** *list, click the disk drive that contains the folder, and then double-click the name of the folder.*

Windows XP opens the My Documents folder.

⑤ Click in the **File name** text box and type the name you want to use for the copy.

Note: *The name you type can be up to 255 characters long, but it cannot include the following characters: < > , ? : " \ *.*

⑥ Click **Save**.

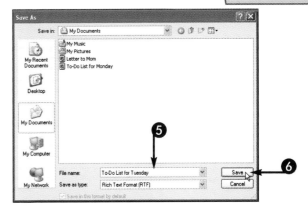

● The file name you typed appears in the program's title bar.

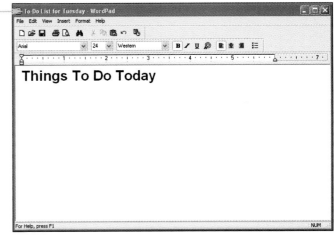

TIP

Can I use the Save As command to make a backup copy of a document?

Yes. Save As can operate as a rudimentary backup procedure. (For a better solution, see the section "Back Up Files" in Chapter 13.) Create a copy with the same name as the original, but store the copy in a different location. Good places to choose are a floppy disk, a second hard drive, or a removable disk. Remember, too, that after you complete the Save As steps, the *copy* will be open in the program. Be sure to close the copy and then reopen the original.

Edit Document Text

When you are working with a character-based file, such as a text or word processing document or an e-mail message, you need to know the basic techniques for editing, selecting, copying, and moving text.

Edit Document Text

DELETE CHARACTERS

① Click immediately to the left of the first character you want to delete.

● The cursor appears before the character.

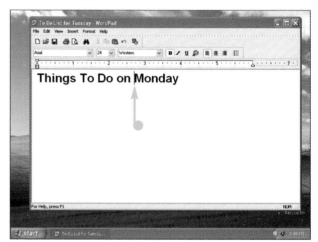

② Press Delete until you have deleted all the characters you want.

Note: *An alternative method is to click immediately to the right of the last character you want to delete and then press* Backspace *until you have deleted all the characters you want.*

Note: *If you make a mistake, immediately click **Edit**, and then click **Undo**. Alternatively, press* Ctrl + Z *or click Undo (* 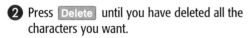 *).*

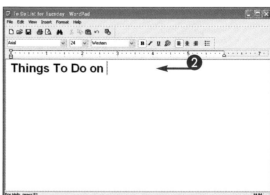

SELECT TEXT FOR EDITING

1 Click and drag across the text you want to select.

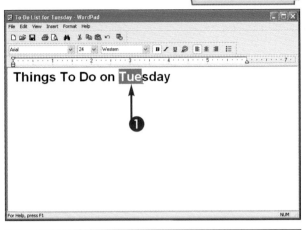

Release the mouse button.

● The program displays the selected text in reverse video.

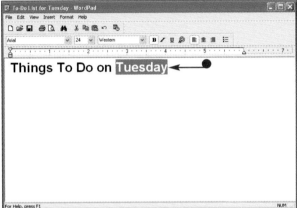

continued

Are there any shortcut methods for selecting text in WordPad?

Yes. Here are the most useful ones:

● Click in the white space to the left of a line to select the line.

● Double-click a word to select it.

● Triple-click inside a paragraph to select it.

● Press Ctrl + A to select the entire document.

Once you select some text, you can work with all of the selected characters together, which is much faster than working with one character at a time. You see some examples in the rest of this section.

Edit Document Text *(continued)*

COPY TEXT

① Select the text you want to copy.

② Click **Edit**.

③ Click **Copy**.

Note: In most programs, you can also press `Ctrl` + `C` *or click Copy (⬚).*

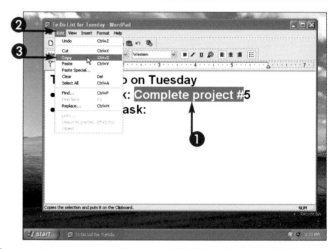

④ Click inside the document at the position where you want the copy of the text to appear.

The cursor appears in the position you clicked.

⑤ Click **Edit**.

⑥ Click **Paste**.

Note: In most programs, you can also press `Ctrl` + `V` *or click Paste (⬚).*

● The program inserts a copy of the selected text at the cursor position.

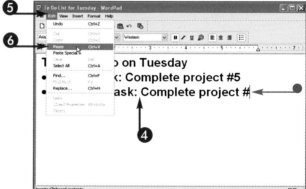

MOVE TEXT

1 Select the text you want to move.

2 Click **Edit**.

3 Click **Cut**.

Note: In most programs, you can also press Ctrl *+* X *or click Cut (✂).*

The program removes the text from the document.

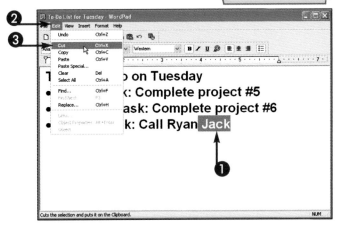

4 Click inside the document at the position where you want to move the text.

The cursor appears at the position you clicked.

5 Click **Edit**.

6 Click **Paste**.

Note: In most programs, you can also press Ctrl *+* V *or click 📋.*

● The program inserts the text at the cursor position.

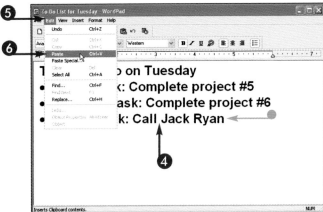

 TIP

How do I move and copy text with my mouse?

First, select the text you want to work with. To move the selected text, place the mouse pointer over the selection, and then click and drag the text to the new position within the document.

To copy the selected text, place the mouse pointer over the selection, hold down the Ctrl key, and then click and drag the text to the desired position within the document.

Change the Text Font

When you work in a word processing document, you can add visual appeal by changing the font formatting.

The font formatting includes attributes such as the typeface (the overall look of each character), style (bold or italic), size, or special effects (such as underline or colors).

① Select the text you want to format.

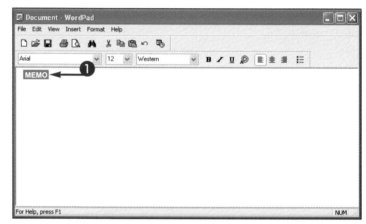

② Click **Format**.

③ Click **Font**.

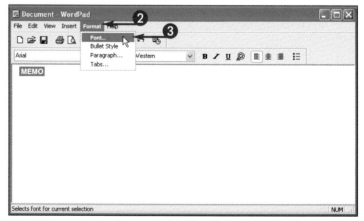

The Font dialog box appears.

Note: The layout of the Font dialog box varies by program, but the one shown here is typical.

④ In the **Font** list, click the typeface you want.

⑤ In the **Font style** list, click the style you want.

⑥ In the **Size** list, click the type size you want.

⑦ In the **Effects** group, click the controls to apply formatting (☐ changes to ☑).

⑧ Click **OK**.

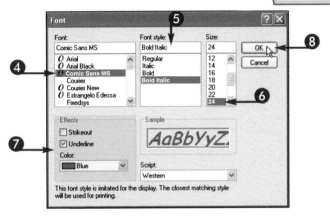

● The program applies the font formatting to the selected text.

Note: Here are some font shortcuts that work in most programs: For bold, press **Ctrl** + **B** *or click Bold (* **B** *); for italics, press* **Ctrl** + **I** *or click Italic (* **/** *); for underline, press* **Ctrl** + **U** *or click Underline (* **U** *).*

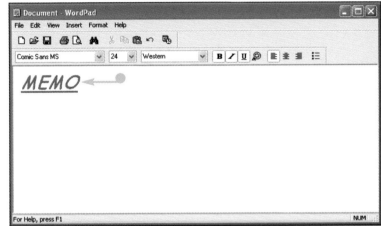

 TIP

How can I make the best use of fonts in my documents?

● Do not use many different typefaces in a single document. Stick to one or at most two typefaces to avoid the "ransom note look."

● Avoid overly decorative typefaces because they are often difficult to read.

● Use bold only for document titles, subtitles, and headings.

● Use italics only to emphasize words and phrases, or for the titles of books and magazines.

● Use larger type sizes only for the document title, subtitle, and possibly the headings.

● If you change the text color, be sure to leave enough contrast between the text and the background. In general, dark text on a light background is the easiest to read.

Find
Text

In large documents, when you need to find specific text, you can save lots of time by using the program's Find feature that searches the entire document in the blink of an eye.

Most programs that work with text – including Windows XP's WordPad and Notepad programs – have the Find feature.

1 Click **Edit**.

2 Click **Find**.

Note: In many programs, you can run the Find command by pressing **Ctrl** + **F** .

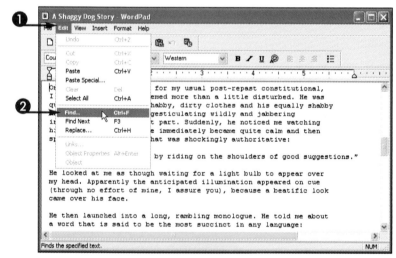

The Find dialog box appears.

3 Click in the **Find what** text box and type the text you want to find.

4 Click **Find Next**.

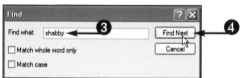

● The program selects the next instance of the search text.

Note: If the search text does not exist in the document, the program displays a dialog box to let you know.

⑤ If the selected instance is not the one you want, click **Find Next** until the program finds the correct instance.

⑥ Click Close (☒) to close the Find dialog box.

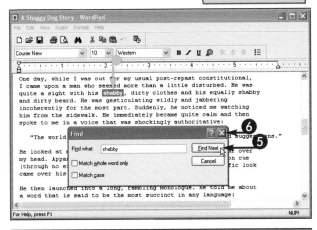

● The program leaves the found text selected.

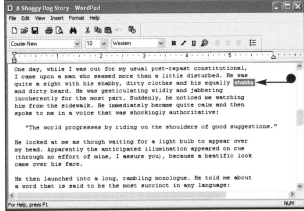

TIPS

When I search for a small word such as *the*, the program matches it in larger words such as *theme* and *bother*. How can I avoid this?

In the Find dialog box, click **Match Whole Word Only** (☐ changes to ☑). This tells the program to match the search text only if it is a word on its own and not part of another word.

When I search for a name such as *Bill*, the program also matches the non-name *bill*. Is there a way to fix this?

In the Find dialog box, click **Match Case** (☐ changes to ☑). This tells the program to match the search text only if it has the same mix of uppercase and lowercase letters that you specify in the **Find what** text box. If you type **Bill**, for example, the program matches only *Bill* and not *bill*.

Do you need to replace a word or part of a word with some other text? If you have several instances to replace, you can save time and do a more accurate job if you let the program's Replace feature replace the word for you.

Most programs that work with text – including Windows XP's WordPad and Notepad programs – have the Replace feature.

Replace Text

① Click **Edit**.

② Click **Replace**.

Note: In many programs, you can run the Replace command by pressing Ctrl + H .

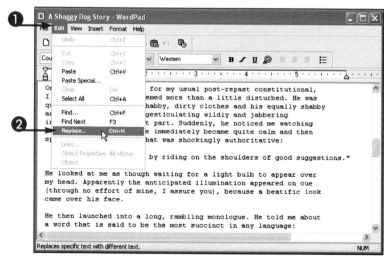

The Replace dialog box appears.

③ In the **Find what** text box, enter the text you want to find.

④ Click in the **Replace with** text box and type the text you want to use as the replacement.

⑤ Click **Find Next**.

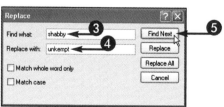

● The program selects the next instance of the search text.

Note: If the search text does not exist in the document, the program displays a dialog box to let you know.

⑥ If the selected instance is not the one you want, click **Find Next** until the program finds the correct instance.

⑦ Click **Replace**.

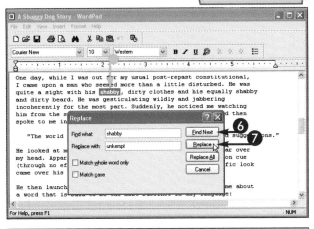

● The program replaces the selected text with the replacement text.

● The program selects the next instance of the search text.

⑧ Repeat steps **6** and **7** until you have replaced all of the instances you want to work with.

⑨ Click ✕ to close the Replace dialog box.

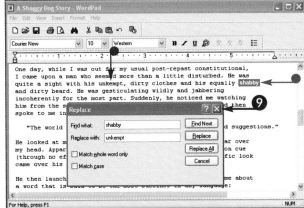

Is there a faster way to replace every instance of the search text with the replacement text?

Yes. In the Replace dialog box, click **Replace All**. This tells the program to replace every instance of the search text with the replacement text. However, you should exercise some caution with this feature because it may make some replacements that you did not intend. Click **Find Next** a few times to make sure the matches are correct. Also, consider using the **Match whole word only** and **Match case** check boxes (☐ changes to ☑), as described in the "Find Text" section of this chapter.

Insert Special Symbols

You can make your documents more readable and more useful by inserting special symbols that are not available via your keyboard.

These special symbols include foreign characters such as ö and é, mathematical symbols such as ÷ and ½, financial symbols such as ¢ and ¥, commercial symbols such as © and ®, and many more.

Insert Special Symbols

① Click **start**.

② Click **All Programs**.

③ Click **Accessories**.

④ Click **System Tools**.

⑤ Click **Character Map**.

The Character Map window appears.

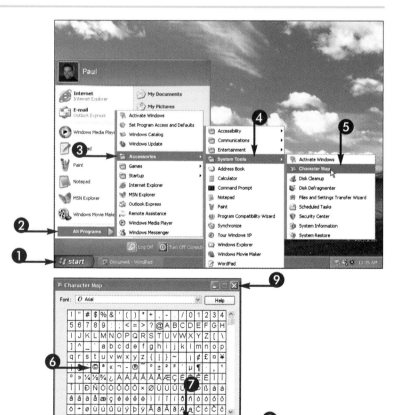

⑥ Click the symbol you want.

*Note: Many other symbols are available in the Webdings and Wingdings typefaces. To see these symbols, click the **Font** ☑, and then click either **Webdings** or **Wingdings**.*

⑦ Click **Select**.

● Character Map adds the symbol to the **Characters to copy** box.

⑧ Click **Copy**.

⑨ Click ☒ to shut down Character Map after you choose all the characters you want.

62

⑩ In your document, position the cursor where you want to insert the symbol.

⑪ Click **Edit**.

⑫ Click **Paste**.

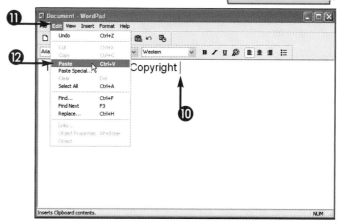

● The program inserts the symbol.

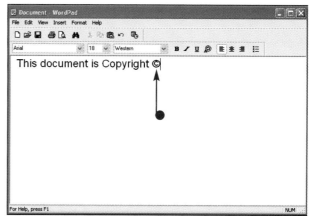

TIP

When I click a symbol, Character Map sometimes displays a Keystroke in the status bar. What does this mean?

This tells you that you can insert the symbol directly into your document by pressing the keystroke shown. For example, you can insert the copyright symbol (©) by pressing Alt + 0 1 6 9. When you type the numbers, be sure to use your keyboard's numeric keypad.

Print a Document

When you need a hard copy of your document, either for your files or to distribute to someone else, you can get a hard copy by sending the document to your printer.

Print a Document

① Turn on your printer.

② Open the document you want to print.

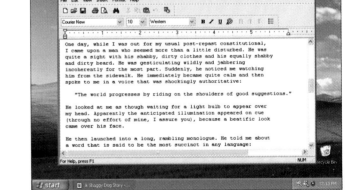

③ Click **File**.

④ Click **Print**.

Note: In many programs, you can select the Print command by pressing **Ctrl** + **P** *or by clicking Print (🖨).*

The Print dialog box appears.

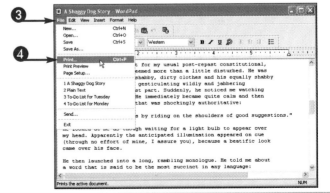

Note: *The layout of the Print dialog box varies from program to program. The WordPad version shown here is a typical example.*

⑤ If you have more than one printer, click the printer you want to use.

⑥ Use the **Number of copies** spin button 🔾 to specify the number of copies to print.

⑦ Click **Print**.

Note: *In many programs, you can send a document directly to the printer by clicking 🖨.*

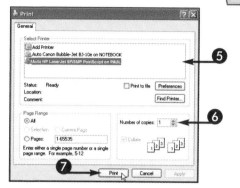

● Windows XP prints the document. The print icon (🖨) appears in the taskbar's notification area while the document prints.

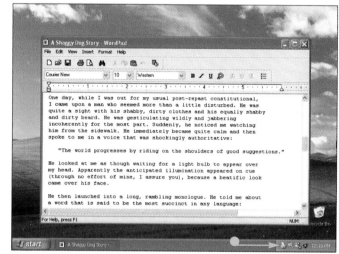

 TIP

How do I print only part of a document?
Most programs enable you to use the following methods to print only part of the document:

● Print selected text: Select the text you want to print. In the Print dialog box, click **Selection** (○ changes to ◉).

● Print a specific page: Place the cursor on the page you want to print. In the Print dialog box, click **Current Page** (○ changes to ◉).

● Print a range of pages: In the Print dialog box, click **Pages** (○ changes to ◉). In the text box, type the first page number, a dash (–), and the last page number (for example, 1-5).

Creating and Working with Images

Whether you load your images from a digital camera or a scanner, download them from the Internet, or draw them yourself, Windows XP comes with a number of useful tools for working with those images.

View Your Images

Before you can work with your images, you need to view them on your computer. You do that by opening Windows XP's My Pictures folder, which is a special folder designed specifically for storing images.

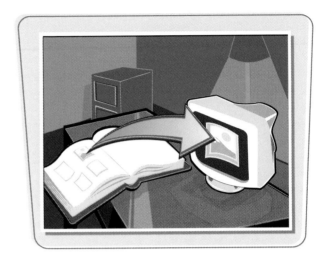

① Click **start**.

② Click **My Pictures**.

The My Pictures folder appears.

③ Double-click the image you want to view.

The image appears in Windows Picture and
Fax Viewer.

④ To get a closer look at the image, click
Zoom In (🔍).

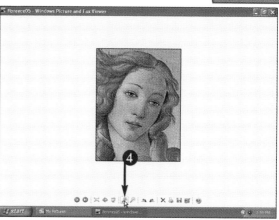

Windows Picture and Fax Viewer zooms in on the
image.

⑤ To see more of the image, click Zoom Out (🔍).

⑥ To preview the next image in the folder, click Next
Image (🔲).

⑦ To preview the previous image in the folder, click
Previous Image (🔲).

⑧ Click Close (✖) to shut down Windows Picture and
Fax Viewer.

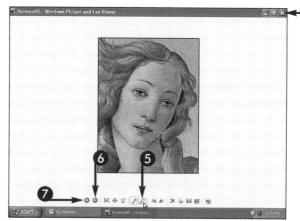

TIP

**I am not sure which file in the My
Pictures folder represents the image
I want to view. How can I find the
image I want?**

The easiest way is to display all the images
as *thumbnails* – scaled-down versions of
the actual images:

① Click **View**.

② Click **Thumbnails**.

● Windows XP displays the images
as thumbnails.

View Images as a Filmstrip

Windows XP enables you to view a group of images as a series of frames in a filmstrip. Unlike the other list view modes, the Filmstrip view mode enables you to see a larger preview of a snapshot alongside a group of snapshots.

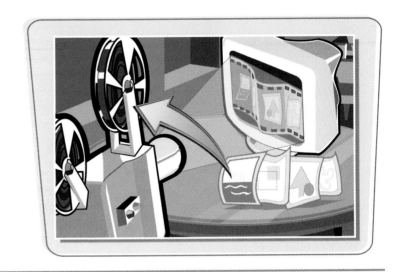

View Images as a Filmstrip

Note: *If you store your snapshots in a special folder within the My Pictures window, open the folder containing the pictures.*

① Click an image in the group of images you want to view in Filmstrip view.

② Click Views (▦▾).

③ Click **Filmstrip**.

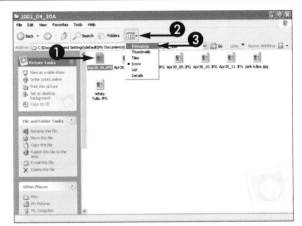

The file list displays the files in Filmstrip view mode.

④ Click here to view another image.

Click ⊙ to advance to the next snapshot.

Click ⊙ to move back to the previous snapshot.

You can also click the image you want to view.

If your image displays sideways, you can click a rotation button to rotate the image in 90-degree increments.

● Click Rotate Clockwise ( ) to rotate the image in a clockwise direction.

● Click Rotate Counterclockwise ( ) to rotate the image in a counterclockwise direction.

● The image rotates in the List view area.

 TIPS

How did my photo end up sideways?

When you take a vertical shot with your digital camera, your photo appears sideways when you download the image to your computer. You may also have scanned the image vertically instead of horizontally. The rotate buttons can help you reposition the image for better viewing.

Can I also use the rotation commands on the shortcut menu?

Yes. If you right-click over an image, the shortcut menu appears and lists the **Rotate Clockwise** and **Rotate Counter Clockwise** commands. You can select either command to rotate the image. You can only view these commands in the shortcut menu while viewing your images in Filmstrip view mode.

Preview
an Image

You can preview any saved image file using the Details feature in the My Pictures folder. The Details feature, located on the left task pane, also displays details about the file, such as the file type, dimensions, and modification date.

You can also use the Details feature to view images stored in _subfolders_ – folders stored within the main My Pictures folder.

Preview an Image

① Click the image file you want to preview.

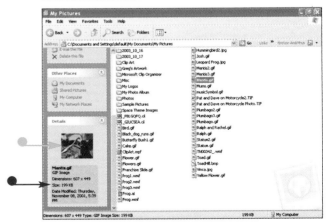

● The Details area of the folder window shows a preview of the image.

Note: _Depending on your screen resolution setting, you may need to scroll down to view the Details area._

● Details about the image file appear here.

You can view the images you store in the My Pictures folder as a slide show. The task pane includes a link to activate the slide show feature. After you start the show, the feature automatically advances and displays each image in the current folder as a slide.

If the folder you want to view holds a lot of photos, the slide show may progress much more slowly than a folder containing just a few files.

View Images as a Slide Show

Note: If you store your snapshots in a special folder within the My Pictures window, open the folder containing the pictures.

① Click **View as a slide show**.

The first photo appears as a slide, and each slide advances automatically.

● You can use the navigation bar in the top-right corner to control the slide show manually.

You can also advance each slide by clicking the screen.

② Click ☒ to exit the slide show.

You can also press **Esc** to exit the slide show.

Scan an Image

You can scan an image using a scanner and store the image on your computer. For example, you can scan a photo to use in a document or to publish later on a Web page. You can use the Scanner and Camera Wizard to guide you through the scanning procedure.

Scanning is just one way that you can import digital images to your computer.

Scan an Image

① Turn on your scanner and position a photo on the scanner bed.

② Click **start**.

③ Click **All Programs**.

④ Click **Accessories**.

⑤ Click **Scanner and Camera Wizard**.

Note: The Scanner and Camera Wizard does not work with all scanners.

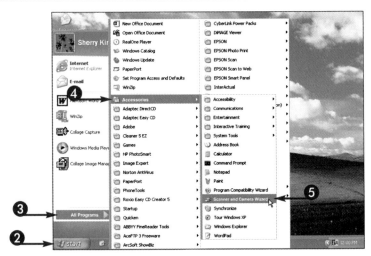

The Scanner and Camera Wizard appears.

⑥ Click **Next**.

The scanning preferences page appears.

⑦ Click the picture type that you want to scan
(○ changes to ◉).

● You can click **Custom settings** to set additional
scan options.

⑧ Click **Preview**.

● A preview of the scanned image appears here.

If you do not like the preview image, you can adjust
the picture in the scanner before proceeding with
the actual scan.

⑨ Click **Next**.

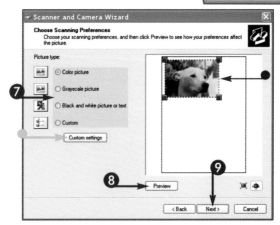

The Picture Name and Destination page appears.

⑩ Type a name for the image.

⑪ Select a file format for the image.

Note: The Scanner and Camera Wizard supports the JPEG, BMP, TIF, and
PNG file formats, with JPEG often as the default selection.

⑫ Select a destination folder for the scan.

● You can click **Browse** and select another folder.

⑬ Click **Next**.

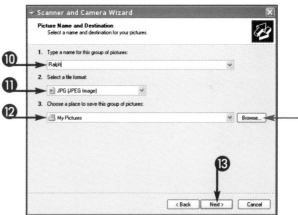

 TIPS

How do I crop an image in the Scanner and Camera Wizard?

In the Choose Scanning
Preferences page in the
wizard, click the **Preview**
button to create a
preview of the scan.
Drag the handles
around the image
preview if you want to
crop your picture to a smaller
size. For example, you may
want to crop out the edges of a
picture so the subject matter receives more
attention.

I cannot activate the Scanner and Camera Wizard. Why not?

Make sure your scanner is
connected properly to
your computer and is
turned on. The
Scanner and Camera
Wizard does not
support all scanners.
If your scanning
device does not
support the WIA
standard, you must use the
proprietary software that comes
with the scanner in order to operate the
device.

continued

After you scan an image, you can specify how you want to work with the image. You can view your newly scanned image in the default My Pictures folder window, or in the folder you designated when determining where to save the picture file.

Scan an Image *(continued)*

The Scanning Picture page appears.

The Scanner and Camera Wizard begins scanning the picture.

● This area displays information about the scan's progress.

● You can click **Cancel** to stop the scan procedure.

The Other Options page appears.

⑭ Select what you want to do with the scanned image (○ changes to ◉).

⑮ Click **Next**.

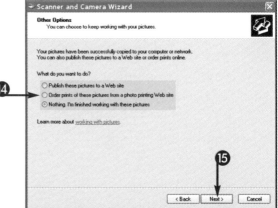

The completion page appears.

16 Click **Finish**.

The Scanner and Camera Wizard closes.

The folder window appears, displaying the newly scanned image.

● The scanned picture's file name appears highlighted in the list view.

17 Click ☒ to close the window when you are finished viewing the picture.

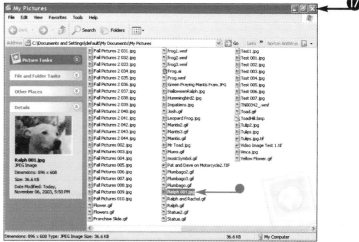

TIPS

How do I view a picture I have previously scanned?

If you store your scanned pictures in the My Pictures folder or in a subfolder within the default folder, you can use the folder window to preview and manage your scanned picture files.

I do not like my scanned picture results. How do I redo the scan?

You can delete the file from the My Pictures folder window and activate the Scanner and Camera Wizard again to rescan the image. You can click **Custom settings** in the second wizard page to open a Properties dialog box and adjust the brightness, contrast, and resolution settings for the scan.

Load an Image from a Digital Camera

You can upload pictures from a digital camera to your computer without using any proprietary software that came with the camera. You can use the Scanner and Camera Wizard to select which photos you want to upload, as well as delete images that you no longer want to store on your camera's storage card.

If you use a card reader device, then you can use these same steps to upload images from the memory or media card without needing to plug in your camera.

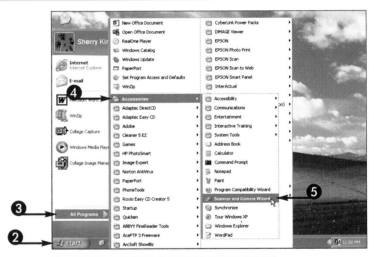

① Plug in your camera or digital storage card reader.

Note: You may need to turn the camera on and activate a mode switch before uploading pictures.

② Click **start**.

③ Click **All Programs**.

④ Click **Accessories**.

⑤ Click **Scanner and Camera Wizard**.

Note: The Scanner and Camera Wizard does not work with all digital cameras.

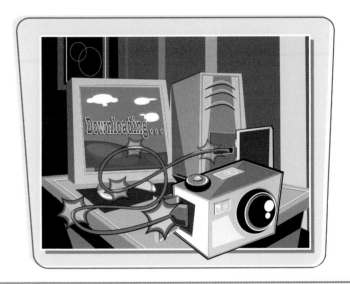

The Scanner and Camera Wizard appears.

⑥ Click **Next**.

A new page appears, displaying thumbnails of your pictures.

7 Click the check box next to any pictures that you want to upload (☐ changes to ☑).

● You can click a check box to deselect a picture you do not want to upload (☑ changes to ☐).

● To rotate a picture, click the picture and click a rotation button.

8 Click **Next**.

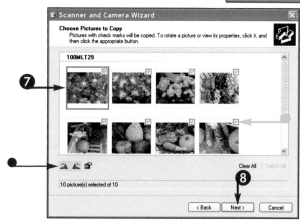

The Picture Name and Destination page appears.

9 Type a name for your group of pictures.

10 Click ☑ to designate a folder to save the pictures to, or leave the default folder selected.

● You can click **Browse** and navigate to another folder to store your pictures.

● If you want to delete the pictures from your camera or memory card after uploading, click this option (☐ changes to ☑).

11 Click **Next**.

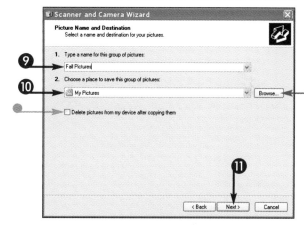

 TIP

I cannot open the Scanner and Camera Wizard. Why not?
Depending on how you set up the software, you may still be able to use the Scanner and Camera Wizard. When you plug in your camera or card reader, a prompt like the one shown here may appear, asking what action you want to perform. One of the options in the list is to use the Microsoft Scanner and Camera Wizard. You can make your selection from the list of options and click **OK**.

continued

By default, Windows XP stores your uploaded pictures in the My Pictures folder, unless you specify another folder. Depending on your computer and the number of pictures you captured on the camera, the uploading process may take a few seconds or several minutes. After you finish the uploading procedure, you can view your pictures in the folder you selected.

Load an Image from a Digital Camera *(continued)*

The Copying Pictures page appears.

The Scanner and Camera Wizard begins to upload pictures from your camera.

● Information about each picture and the upload progress appears here.

● To stop the upload at any time, you can click **Cancel**.

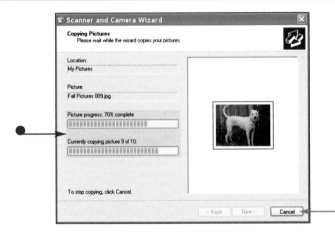

⑫ Select what you want to do with the pictures (○ changes to ◉).

⑬ Click **Next**.

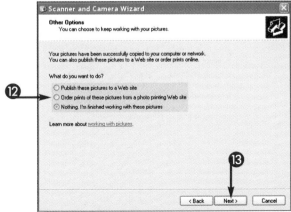

The wizard completion page appears.

⑭ Click **Finish**.

The Scanner and Camera Wizard window closes.

The My Pictures folder window appears automatically and highlights the newly uploaded pictures.

⑮ Click ✕.

The My Pictures folder window closes.

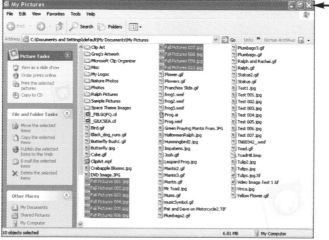

Does the Scanner and Camera Wizard name each of my photos after uploading?

The Scanner and Camera Wizard assigns a common file name to your uploaded pictures, based on the group name you enter. For example, if you typed Vacation as your group name, the wizard names all the pictures you upload with the file name Vacation, followed by individual picture numbers, such as Vacation 001 and Vacation 002.

Print an Image

You can print an image from the My Pictures folder, or from any subfolder in the My Pictures folder. When you activate the Print this Picture task, the Photo Printing Wizard appears. You can follow the steps in the wizard dialog boxes to choose a printer and a layout, and to send the image to the printer.

Print an Image

① Click the image you want to print.

② Click **Print this picture**.

The Photo Printing Wizard appears.

③ Click **Next**.

● The wizard places ☑ next to the image you selected for printing.

● To print additional photos in the current folder, you can click other images you want to include in the printing process (☐ changes to ☑).

④ Click **Next**.

The Printing Options window appears.

● If you use more than one printer with your computer, you can click ⊡ and select which printer you want to use.

5 Click **Next**.

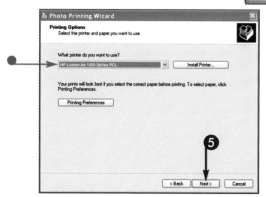

The Layout Selection window appears.

6 Click the layout you want to use for the printed image.

● The wizard displays a preview of the printout.

7 Click **Next**.

The wizard sends your image to the printer.

8 Click **Finish**.

The Photo Printing wizard closes.

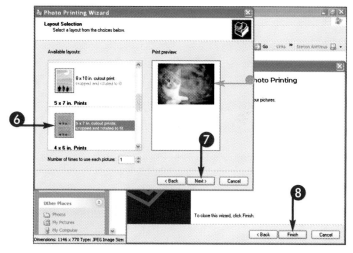

What type of paper should I use for my photo printouts?

Depending on the type of printer you are using, you can find a variety of photo-quality paper types for printing out your digital photographs. Photo-quality paper, though more expensive than multipurpose paper, is designed to create a more permanent image and improve the resolution and color of the printed images. Photo-quality paper comes in glossy and matte finishes, as well as variations of each. Be sure to select a photo-quality paper that your printer manufacturer recommends.

Paint, a program that comes with Windows XP, enables you to draw simple pictures using a variety of tools.

Start Paint

USE THE START MENU

1 Click **start**.

2 Click **All Programs**.

3 Click **Accessories**.

4 Click **Paint**.

● The Paint window appears.

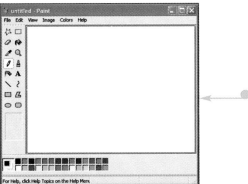

LOAD AN IMAGE INTO PAINT

1. Open the My Pictures folder.
2. Click the image you want to work with.
3. Click **File**.
4. Click **Open With**.
5. Click **Paint**.

Windows XP loads the image into Paint.

TIP

Double-clicking an image opens it in Microsoft Picture and Fax Viewer. How can I get Windows XP to open a double-clicked image in Paint?

1. Click the image you want to open.

2. Click **File**.

3. Click **Open With**.

4. Click **Choose Program**.

   The Open With dialog box appears.

5. Click **Paint**.

6. Click **Always use the selected program to open this kind of file** (☐ changes to ☑).

7. Click **OK**.

Note: Windows XP supports several different types of images, so you may need to repeat these steps for other types of images.

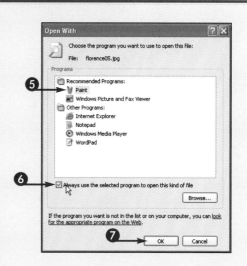

To get the most out of Paint, you need to become familiar with the various tools and features that Paint offers. This section gives you a tour of the Paint window.

Tool Box
The Tool Box contains the tools that you use to draw lines and shapes, add text, and edit the drawing.

Drawing Area
The drawing area is the main area where you create your drawing.

Color Box
The color box displays the available colors that you can use for the drawing tools.

Current Colors
The current colors displays the currently selected foreground color and background color, as represented by the top box and the bottom box, respectively.

Tool Styles
The tool styles area displays the styles that are available for the selected tool. You use these styles to modify how the tool works.

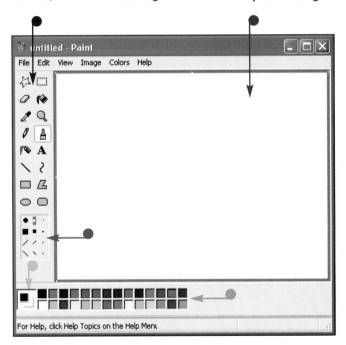

You can create a drawing in Paint. This is useful if you need a specific image but do not have access to or cannot afford a professional illustrator or artist. The next few sections give you specific instructions for each Paint drawing tool.

For example, if you need to design a logo for a project or company, you can use Paint to do it yourself instead of hiring a professional.

Create a Drawing

① Click the tool you want to use.

② If the tool has styles, click the style you want to use.

③ Click a color to set the foreground color.

④ Right-click a color to set the background color.

Note: To choose a color that already exists in the drawing, click the Eyedropper (🖉), and then click the color to set the foreground color, or right-click the color to set the background color.

⑤ Use the mouse to draw the line or shape in the drawing area.

Note: If you make a mistake while adding a shape (or performing any other task in Paint), complete the shape, click **Edit**, and then **Undo** to remove the shape from the drawing.

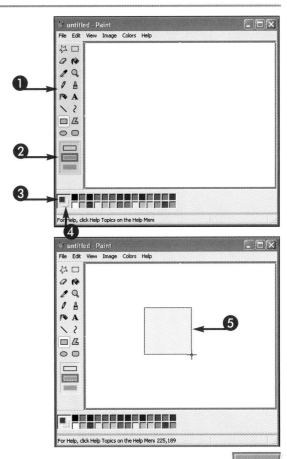

Straight lines of varying lengths and widths are an integral part of any drawing, so you need to know how to create them in Paint.

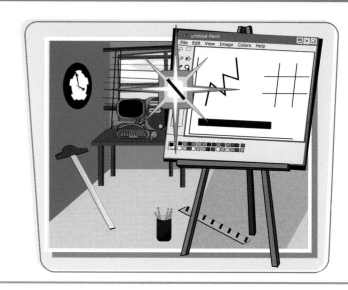

① Click the Line tool (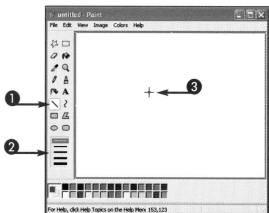) in the Tool Box.

② Click the line style you want to use.

③ Position the mouse pointer inside the drawing area where you want the line to begin (⫭ changes to ⊞).

④ Click and drag the ⊞ until the line is the length you want.

Note: *To draw a line perfectly horizontal, vertical, or at a 45 degree angle, hold down* **Shift** *while you drag the* ⊞.

Note: *To draw the line using the current background color, right-click and drag the* ⊞.

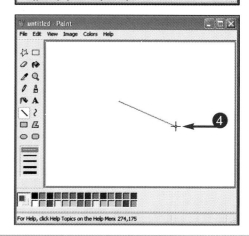

Rectangles and squares are the basic building blocks of any Paint drawing. They not only make useful starting points for drawing objects, but you can also use them to create borders and add details.

Draw a Rectangle

1. Click the Rectangle tool (▣) in the Tool Box.
2. Click the rectangle style you want to use (border only, border with inside color, or no border).
3. Position the mouse pointer inside the drawing area where you want the rectangle to begin (↔ changes to ⊞).

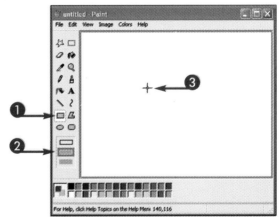

4. Click and drag the ⊞ until the rectangle is the size and shape you want.

Note: To draw a square, hold down **Shift** while you drag the ⊞.

Note: The border uses the current foreground color and the inside color uses the current background color. The no-border style uses the current foreground color. To reverse these colors, right-click and drag the ⊞.

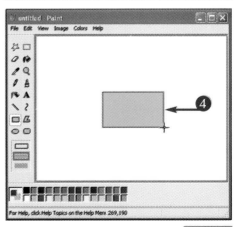

Draw a Rounded Rectangle

If you want a softer look to your rectangles, then you need to use a rounded rectangle, which is a rectangle with its corners rounded off.

Draw a Rounded Rectangle

① Click the Rounded Rectangle tool (🔲) in the Tool Box.

② Click the rounded rectangle style you want to use (border only, border with inside color, or no border).

③ Position the mouse pointer inside the drawing area where you want the rounded rectangle to begin (◌ changes to ⊞).

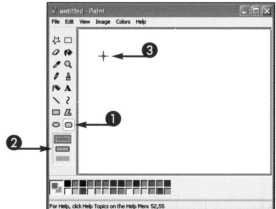

④ Click and drag the ⊞ until the rounded rectangle is the size and shape you want.

Note: *To draw a square, hold down* **Shift** *while you drag the* ⊞.

Note: *The border uses the current foreground color and the inside color uses the current background color. The no-border style uses the current foreground color. To reverse these colors, right-click and drag the* ⊞.

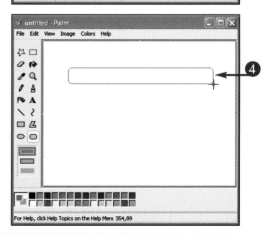

Ellipses of various shapes and sizes are a useful addition to many drawings. And if you need a perfect circle, Paint enables you to draw those, too.

Draw an Ellipse or Circle

① Click the Ellipse tool (⬭) in the Tool Box.

② Click the ellipse style you want to use (border only, border with inside color, or no border).

③ Position the mouse pointer inside the drawing area where you want the ellipse to begin (👆 changes to ✛).

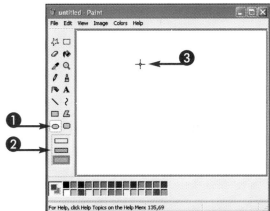

④ Click and drag the ✛ until the ellipse is the size and shape you want.

Note: To draw a circle, hold down **Shift** while you drag the ✛.

Note: The border uses the current foreground color and the inside color uses the current background color. The no-border style uses the current foreground color. To reverse these colors, right-click and drag the ✛.

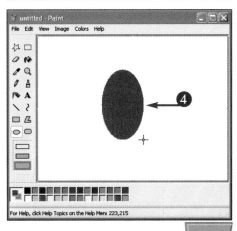

You can use the Curve tool to create arcs, parabolas, sine curves, S shapes, and other kinds of curved lines.

① Click the Curve tool (☑) in the Tool Box.

② Click the line style you want to use.

③ Position the mouse pointer inside the drawing area where you want the curve to begin (⬚ changes to ⊞).

④ Click and drag the ⊞ until the line is the length you want.

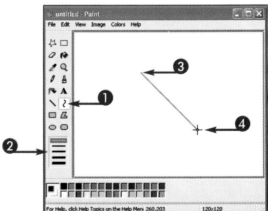

⑤ To curve the line, click and drag the ⊞ until the curve is the shape you want.

⑥ To add a second curve, click and drag the ⊞ until the curve is the shape you want.

Note: To draw the line using the current background color, right-click and drag the ⊞.

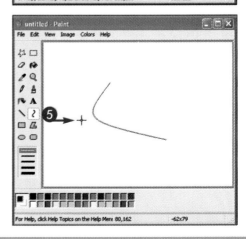

You can use the Polygon tool to draw enclosed objects with three or more sides where each side is a straight line.

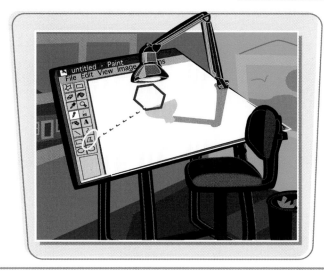

Draw a Polygon

1. Click the Polygon tool (⬜).
2. Click a box style.
3. Position the mouse pointer inside the drawing area where you want the polygon to begin (↖ changes to ✛).
4. Click and drag the ✛ until the first line is the length you want.
5. Position the ✛ at the location where you want the next side to end and click.
6. Repeat step **5** to draw other polygon sides except for the final side.

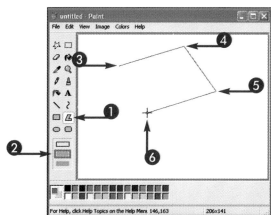

7. For the final side, move the ✛ to the beginning of the first line and click.

   Paint encloses the polygon.

Note: The border uses the current foreground color and the inside color uses the current background color. The no-border style uses the current foreground color. To reverse these colors, right-click and drag the ✛.

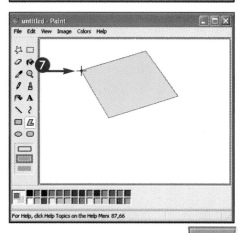

Draw Freehand with a Pencil

When you need a line or shape that just is not possible with the standard Paint tools, then you need to draw the line or shape freehand. You can do this using the Pencil tool.

Draw Freehand with a Pencil

① Click the Pencil tool (✏) in the Tool Box.

② Position the mouse pointer inside the drawing area where you want the shape to begin (⤧ changes to ✏).

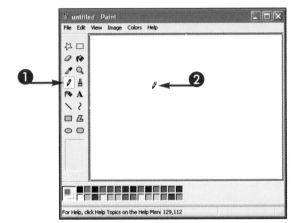

③ Click and drag the ✏ to draw the shape you want.

Note: *To draw the shape using the current background color, right-click and drag the* ✏ *.*

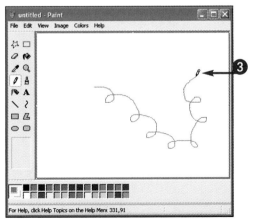

With Paint, you can draw a
freehand line or shape using the
Brush tool, which offers a
variety of styles.

Draw Freehand with a Brush

① Click the Brush tool (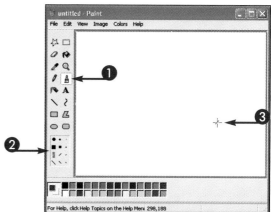) in the Tool Box.

② Click the brush style you want to use.

③ Position the mouse pointer inside the drawing
area where you want the shape to begin (↖ changes
to ⊞).

④ Click and drag the ⊞ to draw the shape you want.

Note: *To draw the shape using the current background color, right-click
and drag the* ⊞ *.*

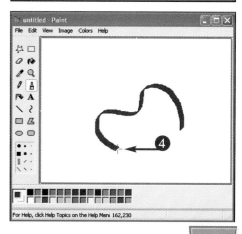

Draw Freehand with an Airbrush

You can create freehand lines and shapes with the Airbrush tool. This "sprays" a color in a variety of styles, much like a can of spray paint.

Draw Freehand with an Airbrush

1 Click the Airbrush tool (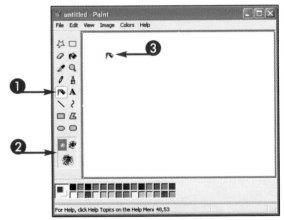) in the Tool Box.

2 Click the Airbrush style you want to use.

3 Position the mouse pointer inside the drawing area where you want the shape to begin (⬚ changes to 🖌).

4 Click and drag the 🖌 to draw the shape you want.

Note: To draw the shape using the current background color, right-click and drag the 🖌 .

Note: The slower you drag the 🖌 , the more the paint spreads and the more saturated the spray becomes.

Fill a Shape with Color

You can use the Fill With Color tool to fill any enclosed shape with the color you choose.

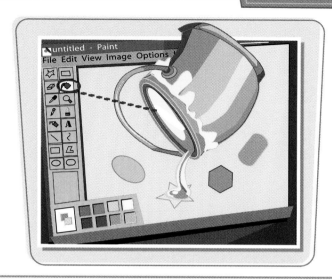

① Click the Fill With Color tool () in the Tool Box.

② Click the color you want to use.

③ Position the mouse pointer inside the shape you want to fill (▷ changes to).

④ Click.

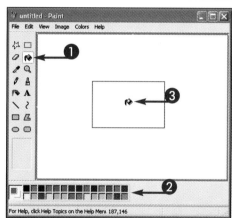

● Paint fills the shape with the foreground color.

Note: If you want to fill a shape with the background color, with the 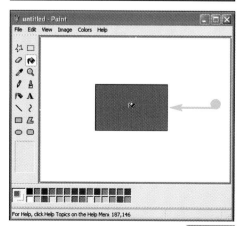
positioned inside the shape, right-click.

Add Text

If you need to add a title, caption, annotation, or other text to your drawing, you can do this using the Text tool, which also enables you to use different text typefaces, styles, and sizes.

Add Text

① Click the Text tool (🔠) in the Tool Box.

② Click the Text style you want to use (opaque or transparent background).

③ Position the mouse pointer inside the drawing area where you want the text to begin (⬚ changes to ⊞).

④ Click and drag the ⊞ to create a box big enough to hold the text.

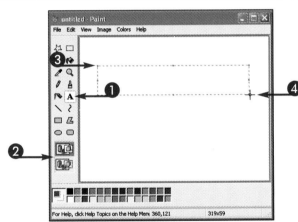

Paint displays the Fonts toolbar.

⑤ Use the controls in the Fonts toolbar to choose the typeface, size, and style for the text.

⑥ Click in the text box and type the text.

⑦ Click outside the box to set the text.

Note: After you set the text, you cannot edit it. Therefore, before setting the text, double-check your spelling and your font settings to ensure they are correct.

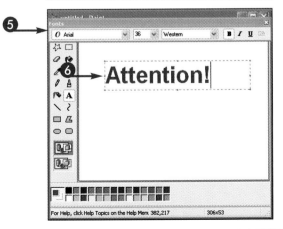

You can use the Pick Color tool to pick any color from the drawing. This enables you to work with a color that is not represented in the color box.

Pick a Color

1 Click the Pick Color tool () in the Tool Box.

2 Position the mouse pointer over the color you want to pick (↖ changes to ✎).

3 Click.

● Paint sets the color as the current foreground color.

Note: If you want the color you pick to become the current background color, with the ✎ positioned over the color, right-click.

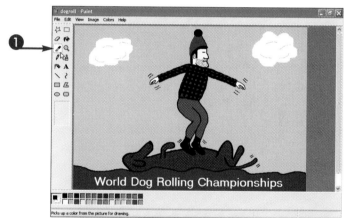

Use the Eraser

If there are parts of your drawing that you do not like or do not need, instead of starting over, you can save time by erasing only those parts of the drawing that you do not want in the finished image.

You can use Paint's Eraser tool in two different ways: to erase lines, shapes, and colors, or to erase only a specified color.

ERASE LINES, SHAPES, AND COLORS

① Click the Eraser tool () in the Tool Box.

② Click the Eraser style you want to use (this sets the size of the eraser).

③ Right-click the white square in the Color Box to set the Eraser tool's color.

④ Position the mouse pointer inside the drawing area where you want to begin erasing (⊿ changes to ▣).

⑤ Click and drag the ▣ over the area you want to erase.

Paint erases everything in the path of the ▣.

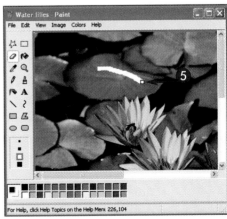

ERASE A COLOR

① Click in the Tool Box.

② Click the Eraser style you want to use (this sets the size of the eraser).

③ Click the color you want to erase in the Color Box.

④ Right-click the white square in the Color Box.

⑤ Position the mouse pointer inside the drawing area where you want to begin erasing (⥀ changes to ▣).

⑥ Right-click and drag the ▣ over the area with the color you want to erase.

Paint erases the color in the path of the ▣.

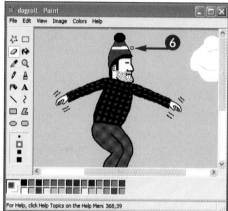

TIP

How can I replace one color with another?

When you use the Eraser tool, it actually replaces everything in its path with the currently selected background color. So when you set the background color to white, the Eraser tool effectively erases everything in its path. However, when you right-click and drag the ▣, the Eraser tool looks for only the current foreground color and replaces it with the current background color. Therefore, to replace one color with another, click the color you want replaced and right-click the color you want to use as the replacement.

CHAPTER 5

Playing Music and Other Media

Using Windows Media Player, you can listen to audio files, music CDs, and Internet radio stations, watch video files, play DVD discs, and even create your own music CDs.

Open and Close
Windows Media Player

Windows XP includes Windows Media Player to enable you to play back and record audio as well as to view video. To begin using the program, you must first learn how to find and open the Windows Media Player window. When you finish using the program, you can close the Windows Media Player window to free up computer processing power.

Open and Close Windows Media Player

OPEN WINDOWS MEDIA PLAYER

1. Click **start**.
2. Click **All Programs**.
3. Click **Windows Media Player**.

● The Windows Media Player window appears, displaying the Media Guide page.

Note: You may need to connect to the Internet in order to view all the Media Guide page links.

By default, the Windows Media Player window appears at a reduced size in Full mode. You can resize or maximize the window.

4. Click Show Menu Bar (▣).

A regular menu bar appears, with a regular window border around the Windows Media Player window.

● You can click Hide Menu Bar () to hide the window border again.

CLOSE WINDOWS MEDIA PLAYER

① Click **File**.

② Click **Exit**.

● You can also click Close (⊠) to close the window.

The Windows Media Player window closes.

TIPS

Can I leave Windows Media Player open while I work with other programs?

Yes. You can minimize the Windows Media Player window to run in the background while you work with other programs or tasks. You can also use the new Mini Player toolbar to keep the program open, but minimized to a playback toolbar on your Windows XP desktop taskbar. To activate the Mini Player toolbar, minimize the Windows Media Player window, right-click the toolbar, click **Toolbars**, and then click **Windows Media Player**.

How do I find the latest version of Windows Media Player?

To check which version of the program you have, click the **Help** menu and then **About Windows Media Player**. To upgrade to the latest version, click **Help,** and then **Check for Player Updates**. You can then connect to the Internet and download the latest program version.

When you view Windows Media Player in Full mode, you can access all of the program's features. Familiarizing yourself with the onscreen elements is a good idea so that you can easily navigate and activate elements when you are ready to play audio files or view videos and DVDs.

Title Bar
The title bar displays the name of the program.

Menu Bar
The menu bar displays menus which, when clicked, reveal commands for managing your multimedia items.

Quick Access Box
When clicked, this box displays a menu of other playlists and media sources that you can select to play.

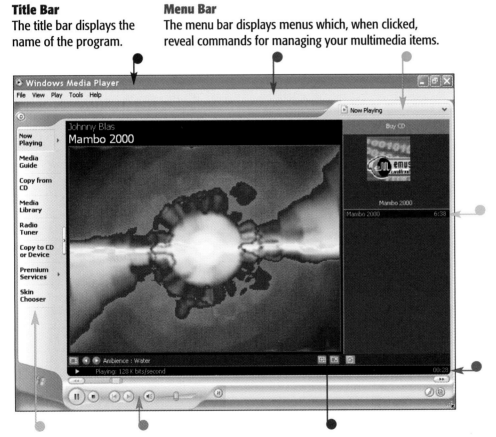

Playlist Pane
The playlist pane displays the individual tracks of a CD or DVD, or any song names in a customized playlist.

Media Information Pane
This pane displays a subset of information about the current content, such as the album art and title.

Features Taskbar
The features taskbar, which is located on the left side of the window, lists tab links to key features.

Playback Controls
These buttons control how a video or music file plays, and enable you to make adjustments to the sound.

Video/Visualization Pane
This pane displays the current video. For audio, it displays visualizations or information about the song.

You can change the size of the Windows Media Player window to free up space on your desktop. For example, you can switch to Skin, or Compact, mode to reduce the Windows Media Player window to a smaller size that displays a graphical theme.

Skin mode does not offer access to all Windows Media Player features, but it offers a convenient way to listen to music in the background as you work with other programs on your computer. You can switch back to Full mode to access all the Windows Media Player features again.

Change the Media Player Window Size

① Click Switch to Skin Mode (⊡).

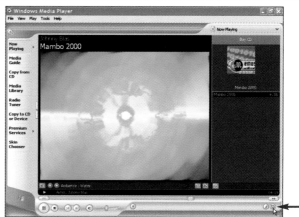

The Windows Media Player window switches to Skin mode.

You can drag the Skin mode window to where you want it on the desktop.

② Click Return to Full Mode (⊞).

The Windows Media Player window switches back to Full mode.

Using the Media Library

You can use the Media Library feature in Windows Media Player to manage all of the media files on your computer, including audio files that you listen to with Windows Media Player. The Media Library also enables you to organize links to other digital content, such as music on the Internet.

Using the Media Library

SEARCH FOR FILES

1 Click the **Media Library** tab.

2 Click **Tools**.

3 Click **Search for Media Files**.

Note: The first time you open the Media Library, a dialog box appears, prompting you to search for multimedia files. Click Yes to conduct the search automatically.

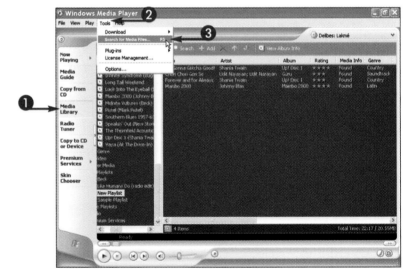

4 Click ⊡ and specify which folder or drive you want to search, or you can search the default selections.

5 Click **Search**.

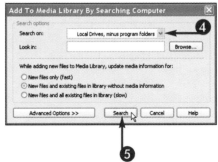

A dialog box appears, displaying the progress of the search.

⑥ When the search is complete, click **Close**.

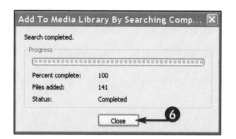

VIEW FILES

● The Contents pane displays expandable and collapsible categories for viewing files in the list.

⑦ Click the category icon (⊞) to expand a category.

You can click the category icon (⊟) to collapse a category.

● The Details pane displays file names and information.

⑧ Double-click a file name to play the file.

You can drag a border to resize a pane to display more or less information.

 TIPS

My Media Library is quite large. How do I search for a specific file?

Click **Search** at the top of the Media Library page. A Search toolbar appears. Type your search criteria or keyword, and then click **Find Now**. Search results appear in the Search Results playlist.

How does the Media Library determine what category to use for a multimedia file?

Files are automatically grouped into the categories based on their media content information. Media content information, also called *metadata* or *tags*, includes information such as the artist name, song title, rating, play count, and composer. Media content information also identifies the file type.

Play an Audio or Video File

Windows Media Player uses the Media Library to play audio files that you store on your computer. When you select an audio file from the Media Library list and play it in Windows Media Player, you can also switch to the Now Playing page to view a visualization along with the song.

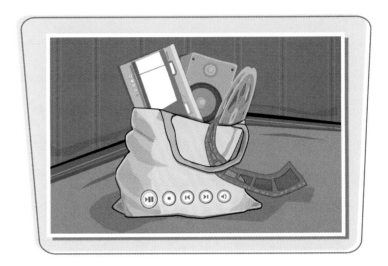

Play an Audio or Video File

1 Click the **Media Library** tab.

2 Open the folder containing the audio or video file that you want to play.

3 Click the audio or video file name.

Note: See the section "Using the Media Library" to learn more about expanding and collapsing categories and viewing files.

4 Click Play (⊙).

Windows Media Player begins playing the audio or video file.

● You can click the **Now Playing** tab to view a visualization with an audio file.

● You can use the playback buttons to control how the song or video plays.

Adjust the Volume

You can adjust the volume in Windows Media Player up or down to get the audio just right.

Adjust the Volume

TURN VOLUME UP OR DOWN

1 Click and drag the **Volume** slider left (to reduce the volume) or right (to increase the volume).

MUTE THE VOLUME

1 Click Mute (🔊).

Note: *To restore the volume, click Sound (🔊).*

Play a Music CD

You can play your favorite music CDs in Windows Media Player. The Now Playing page displays the individual tracks on the CD in the Playlist pane, and the Video/Visualization pane pulsates with the musical beats as the CD plays.

Play a Music CD

PLAY A CD

① Insert a CD into your computer's CD-ROM drive.

The Audio CD dialog box appears.

Note: See the section "Play an Audio or Video File" earlier in this chapter to learn how to play audio and video files that you store on your computer.

② Click **Play audio CD using Windows Media Player**.

③ Click **OK**.

The Windows Media Player window appears and begins playing the first song.

● This area displays the current visualization.

● The playlist displays each song on the CD, along with the song length.

● On commercial CDs, the album title appears here.

● You can drag the **Seek** slider () to play a specific part of a song.

SKIP A TRACK

④ Click Next ( ) to skip to the next track.

⑤ Click Previous ( ) to skip to the previous track.

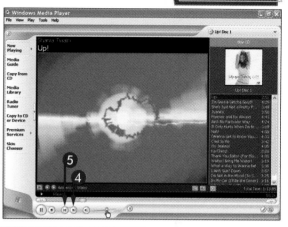

PAUSE PLAY

⑥ Click Pause ( ).

Windows Media Player pauses playback.

 TIPS

How do I repeat an audio CD?

To repeat an audio CD, press Alt to display the menus, click **Play**, and then click **Repeat**. You can also press Ctrl + T.

Can I change visualizations during playback?

Yes. You can click Previous Visualization ( ) or Next Visualization ( ) to quickly switch between the available visualization schemes in Windows Media Player.

continued

You can use the playback
buttons at the bottom of the
Windows Media Player window
to control how a CD plays. For
example, you can stop a CD and
then select another song to play,
or you can pause play if you
have to leave the computer.

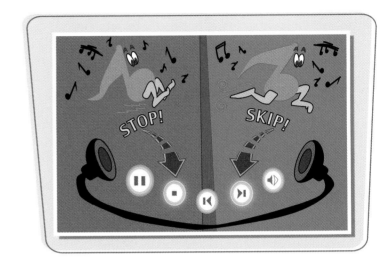

Play a Music CD *(continued)*

RESUME PLAY

⑦ Click ⊙.

Windows Media Player resumes playback where you
left off.

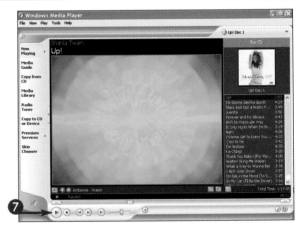

STOP PLAY

⑧ Click Stop (⊡).

Windows Media Player stops playback.

If you click ⊙ after clicking ⊡, the current song
starts over again.

PLAY ANOTHER SONG

9 In the Playlist pane, double-click the song you want to play.

Windows Media Player begins playing the song.

● The current song title appears here.

PLAY SONGS RANDOMLY

10 Click Turn Shuffle On ( ).

Windows Media Player shuffles the order of play.

My Playlist pane does not list the song titles. Why not?

When you play a music CD, Windows Media Player tries to gather information about the album encoded in the CD. However, if it cannot ascertain song titles, then it displays track numbers instead. To type a song title, select the track number, right-click the track, and click **Edit** from the pop-up menu. Windows Media Player highlights the song in the playlist. Type a song title and press **Enter**. You can also press **F2** to edit a song title.

Can I make the same CD play over and over again?

Yes. Click the **Play** menu, then click **Repeat**. Windows Media Player places a check mark next to the command name to indicate the feature is active. This Repeat command tells Windows Media Player to start playing the album over again. To turn the Repeat feature off again, open the **Play** menu and click **Repeat**.

You can use Windows Media Player to play DVDs. If you have a DVD driver and decoder software, you can use the Windows Media Player window to watch any multimedia items stored on a DVD, such as movies and video footage.

Depending on how you set up your DVD drive and Windows Media Player, your DVD may begin playing as soon as you insert it. If not, you can follow the steps in this section to initiate playback.

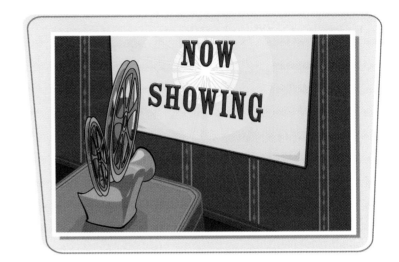

Play a DVD

1. Insert a DVD into your computer's DVD drive.
2. Launch the Windows Media Player.
3. Click **Play**.
4. Click **DVD, VCD, or CD Audio**.
5. Click your DVD drive's name.

- Windows Media Player begins to play the DVD and displays the built-in menu.

   DVD menu items can vary in appearance, and can use different layouts.

6. Click the menu item or feature you want to play.

- Windows Media Player begins playback.

- The tracks appear in the Playlist pane.

- Information – if available – about the DVD appears here, and in the case of commercial DVDs, the cover image also appears.

7 When you finish watching the DVD, click ▣ to exit the Windows Media Player window.

My DVD does not play. Why is this?

Windows Media Player does not include any DVD decoder software. A computer already equipped with a DVD-ROM drive likely has a DVD decoder. However, you may need to purchase a DVD decoder pack add-in for your DVD drive. To search online for a decoder plug-in, follow these steps:

1 In the Windows Media Player window, click **View**.

2 Click **Plug-ins**.

3 Click **Download Plug-ins**.

Your browser window opens and displays a list of plug-in categories for the Windows Media Player.

4 Click the **DVD Decoder Plug-ins** link.

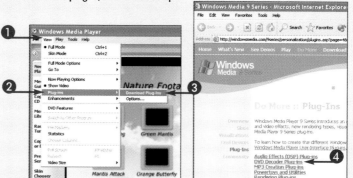

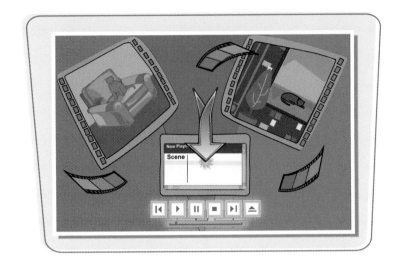

You can control how a DVD plays by using the various navigation controls in the Windows Media Player window. The window includes volume and playback controls. You can also navigate to different scenes using the list of tracks in the Playlist pane. All scenes, or tracks, stem from a root menu that directs you to the DVD's contents.

Navigate a DVD

STOP AND START A DVD

1 Click ▣.

Windows Media Player stops the DVD playback.

2 Click ▶.

Windows Media Player restarts the playback from the beginning.

You can also click ⏸ to pause the playback if you want to resume playing in the same scene.

NAVIGATE SCENES

1 Click ▣.

Windows Media Player jumps you to the previous scene.

2 Click ▣.

Windows Media Player jumps you to the next scene.

● You can also navigate directly to a scene in the playlist by double-clicking the scene you want to play.

RETURN TO THE ROOT MENU

① Click **View**.

② Click **DVD Features**.

③ Click **Root Menu**.

The DVD's opening menu appears in the Windows Media Player window.

 TIPS

What is a root menu?

The root menu is the opening menu of a DVD, typically displaying links to the various segments, features, or clips on the DVD. You can return to the root menu at any time to access other elements on the DVD. You can quickly access the root menu with a shortcut menu. Right-click over the DVD screen, click **DVD Features**, and then click **Root Menu**.

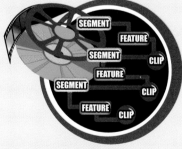

Can I adjust the DVD's play speed?

Yes. You can choose from three settings: Slow, Normal, or Fast. The slow setting plays the DVD in slow motion. The normal setting plays the DVD at normal speed. The fast setting accelerates the play. To change the play speed, click **Play**, click **Play Speed**, and then select a speed. Windows Media Player selects the normal setting by default.

Copy Tracks from a Music CD

You can add tracks from a music CD to the Media Library in Windows Media Player. This enables you to listen to an album without having to put the CD into your CD-ROM drive each time. The process of adding tracks from a CD is called *copying*, or *ripping*, in Windows XP.

The Media Library helps you to organize and manage audio files on your computer. After you add a music track, you can play it from the Media Library page.

Copy Tracks from a Music CD

① Insert a CD into your computer's CD-ROM drive.

② Click the **Copy from CD** tab.

③ Select the CD tracks that you want to copy.

By default, all the tracks are selected for copying. To deselect a track that you do not want to copy, click the check box next to the song title (☑ changes to ☐).

④ Click **Copy Music**.

Windows Media Player displays a dialog box the first time you copy a music CD.

● Click here if you want to play the songs on other computers (☐ changes to ☑).

⑤ Click **OK**.

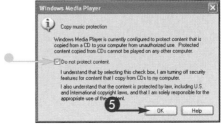

Windows Media Player begins copying the track or tracks.

● The Copy Status column displays the copy progress.

● After each file is copied, the Copy Status column displays a Copied to Library message.

 TIPS

How do I remove an item from the Media Library?

Select the file that you want to remove in the Media Library page, and then click Delete (☒). Select a deletion option from the following: **Delete from Playlist**, **Delete from Library**, or **Delete Playlist**. To permanently remove the file from the Media Library, click **Delete from Library**.

Does the Media Library store information about albums that I copy?

Yes. To view album information, first select the album in the Contents pane of the Media Library page. Then, click View Album Info (▣). The Details pane displays any detailed album information that is available.

A *playlist* is a collection of songs, or music tracks, copied from a music CD, stored on your computer hard drive, or downloaded from the Internet. You can create customized playlists in Windows Media Player that play only the songs that you want to hear.

Create a Playlist

① Click the **Media Library** tab.

② Click **Playlists**.

③ Click **New Playlist**.

The New Playlist dialog box appears.

④ Click the **View Media Library by** ▼.

⑤ Click the category containing the songs you want to add.

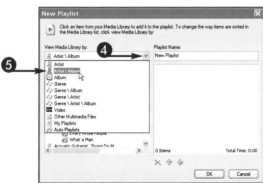

6 Click an item to expand it, and select the song you want to add.

● Windows Media Player adds the song to the playlist.

7 Repeat steps **5** and **6** to add more songs to the playlist.

8 When you finish creating the list, click **OK**.

Windows Media Player adds the playlist to the My Playlists category in the Media Library.

9 Click the playlist name to highlight it.

10 Click the playlist name again to edit the name.

11 Type a new name for the list.

12 Press **Enter**.

Windows Media Player saves the new name.

 TIPS

Can I add items to a playlist?

Yes. Right-click the item that you want to add in the Media Library page, and click **Add to Playlist**. The Add to Playlist dialog box appears. Click the playlist to which you want to add the item and click **OK**.

What does the Queue-It-Up button do?

You can use Queue-It-Up ( ) to temporarily add entire albums, artist lists, and other playlists to a playlist. While playing the playlist, click the **Media Library** tab, click the item that you want to add, and then click .

Burn Music Files to a CD

You can copy, or *burn*, music files from your computer onto a CD. Burning CDs is a great way to create customized CDs that you can listen to on the computer or in a portable device. You can burn music files from within the Windows Media Player window.

Burn Music Files to a CD

① Insert a blank CD into your computer's CD-R or CD-RW drive.

② Launch Windows Media Player.

③ Click the **Copy to CD or Device** tab.

④ Click the **Playlists** ⊡.

⑤ Click the playlist that you want to copy.

Windows Media Player displays the songs.

⑥ Click to deselect any songs that you do not want to burn to the CD (☑ changes to ☐).

By default, Windows Media Player selects all the songs on the playlist for copying.

⑦ Click ⊡.

⑧ Click the CD drive to which you want to copy.

⑨ Click **Copy**.

● Windows Media Player converts the files to CDA format and copies them to the CD.

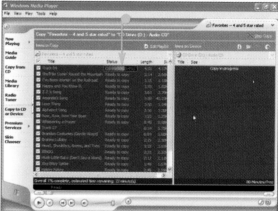

Can I burn files from the My Music folder?

Yes. Select the tracks that you want to copy from your computer to the music CD, and click the **Copy to audio CD** link in the Music Tasks pane of the My Music folder window. When you activate this link, the Windows Media Player window appears, and you can use the Copy to CD or Device tab to copy the files.

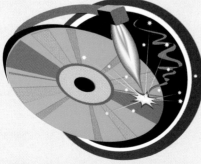

My computer came installed with another CD-burning program. Can I use it instead?

Yes. Although Windows Media Player is good for recording WMA file types, there are other good burner programs for creating CDs for MP3 files. For example, Easy CD Creator (www.roxio.com) and NeroMIX (www.ahead.de) are two very popular audio-burning programs you can use. Check your CD-burning documentation to see if it contains the options and features that match what you want to do.

Using the Media Guide

You can use the Media Guide page in Windows Media Player to access the latest music, movie links, and news on the Internet. The Media Guide is actually a Web page that updates regularly with new information and links. You can use the page to download and listen to audio and video files.

Using the Media Guide

① Click the **Media Guide** tab.

Note: You must connect to the Internet in order to view the Media Guide Web page.

② Click a link.

The Media Guide may display another Web page with more links to explore.

A dialog box may appear, prompting you to obtain a license to play the song.

To obtain a license, you may have to register or pay a fee to listen to the song.

③ Click **Yes** to acquire a license.

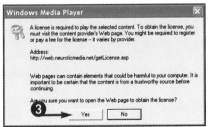

The License Acquisition dialog box appears.

4 Fill out the registration form.

5 Click **Submit**.

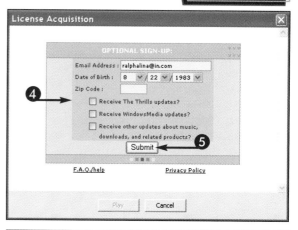

6 Click **Play**.

Windows Media Player begins playing the song.

You can close any additional Web pages that appear and click the **Now Playing** tab in Windows Media Player to listen to the song.

Windows Media Player adds the downloaded song to the Media Library where you can play it anytime.

 TIPS

When I click an audio link, a Media Bar Settings dialog box appears. What should I do?

The Media Bar Settings dialog box asks if you want to play the audio or video file from within the Internet Explorer Web browser window. Click **No** to listen to or view the file in Windows Media Player instead.

How do I navigate the Media Guide pages?

You can click Back and Forward (and) at the top of the Media Guide page to navigate between pages. You can click Home ( ) to return to the home page — the page that first appears when you click the **Media Guide** tab. You can click Refresh ( ) to refresh a page's content. You can click Stop ( ) to stop loading a page.

Listen to Internet Radio

You can quickly tune into an Internet radio station using Windows Media Player. The player includes a variety of *preset channels* or *stations*, which are links to featured radio stations. You can find links to classical, jazz, rock, and talk radio stations.

To listen to an online radio station, you must first log onto your Internet connection and be using a computer with sound capabilities.

Listen to Internet Radio

① Open the Windows Media Player.

② Click the **Radio Tuner** tab.

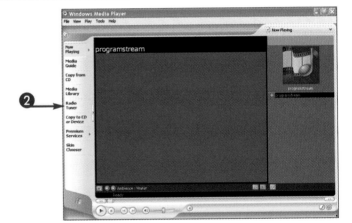

Windows Media Player opens the Radio Tuner page and lists featured stations.

③ Click a station you want to listen to.

● Windows Media Player displays a description of the station and several links.

④ Click the **Play** link.

Note: If the featured station does not offer a Play link, see the tip above.

Windows Media Player connects you to the station and starts playing.

● This area of the window displays connecting information.

A browser window may also appear and display more information about the station.

● You can click ⏹ to stop receiving the broadcast.

⑤ To finish listening to the station and exit the Windows Media Player window, click ✕.

 TIPS

I do not see a Play link. How do I play the station?

You can click the **Visit Website to Play** link to visit the station's Web site and listen to the station through your Web browser. You can find a link to play the station on the station's Web site. Some stations require additional information from you before allowing you to listen to the broadcast.

How do I adjust the volume?

You can either click ◉ to mute the broadcast, or click and drag the **Volume** slider to increase or decrease the volume. If the volume is too quiet with the slider all the way to the right, which is its maximum setting, consider raising the volume with the controls on your computer speakers themselves.

You can customize the Now Playing page in Windows Media Player by hiding or displaying various features. By default, all of the features appear on the page. You can hide items that you do not want to view, or hide features that you are not currently using. For example, you can hide the Playlist pane to view more of the Video/Visualization pane.

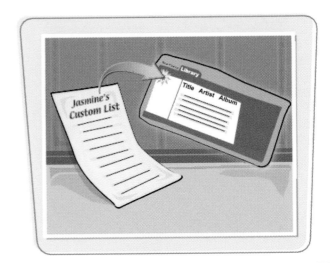

Customize the Now Playing Page

① Click the **Now Playing** features tab.

② Click **View**.

③ Click **Now Playing Options**.

④ Click the feature that you want to hide.

A ☑ appears next to the name of active features. No check mark indicates the feature is hidden.

Windows Media Player hides the feature.

● In this example, the Playlist pane is no longer visible onscreen.

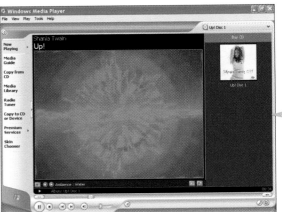

When you use Windows Media Player in Skin mode, you can choose from a variety of graphical themes to give the Windows Media Player window a unique appearance. A *skin* is simply an interface that controls the appearance of the Windows Media Player window and its features.

Windows Media Player offers you a selection of over 20 skins. You can also download more skins from the Windows Media Web site.

Change the Windows Media Player Skin

① Click the **Skin Chooser** tab.

Note: You must switch to Full mode to view the feature tabs. See the section "Change the Media Player Window Size" earlier in the chapter to learn more about switching modes.

② Click a skin to view an example of the interface.

③ When you have selected the skin that you want, click **Apply Skin**.

Windows Media Player switches to Skin mode and displays the skin you selected.

● You can click [⊞] to return to Full mode again.

CHAPTER 6

Working with Files

This chapter shows you how to work with the files on your computer. These easy and efficient methods show you how to view, select, copy, move, rename, and delete files, as well as how to copy files to a CD and how to create new folders to hold your files.

View Your Files

You can view the files you create, as well as those you download and copy to your computer that are stored on your hard drive. If you want to open or work with those files, you first need to view them.

VIEW FILES IN MY DOCUMENTS

1. Click **start**.
2. Click **My Documents**.

Windows XP displays the My Documents window.

3. If the files you want to view are stored in a subfolder, double-click the subfolder.

VIEW FILES IN A FLOPPY, CD, OR REMOVABLE DISK DRIVE

1 Insert the floppy, CD, or removable disk into the drive.

2 Click **start**.

3 Click **My Computer**.

Windows XP displays the My Computer window.

4 Double-click the disk drive that contains the files you want to view.

My Computer displays the contents of the disk drive.

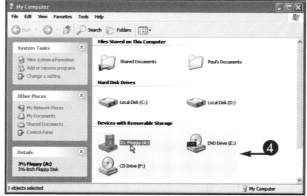

 TIP

When I open drive C, Windows XP displays a message telling me that its files are hidden. Is it okay to view these files?

Yes, but only if you know exactly where the files you want to view are located. Drive C contains all the *system files* that keep Windows XP running. If you accidentally move, rename, or delete any of these files, Windows XP may run erratically or crash. In general, it is much safer to stick with the My Documents folder or other disk drives, such as floppy, CD, and removable drives. If you decide to view the contents of drive C, click **Show the contents of this folder**.

Whether you want to rename a file, move several files to a new location, or delete some files, you first have to select the files so that Windows XP knows exactly which ones you want to work with.

Although you learn specifically about selecting files in this section, the technique for selecting folders is exactly the same.

Select a File

SELECT A SINGLE FILE

1 Open the folder containing the file.

2 Click the file.

SELECT MULTIPLE FILES

1 Open the folder containing the files.

2 Click the first file you want to select.

3 Hold down `Ctrl` and click each of the other files you want to select.

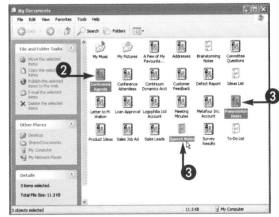

SELECT A GROUP OF FILES

1 Open the folder containing the files.

2 Position the mouse pointer (🖑) slightly above and slightly to the left of the first file in the group.

3 Click and drag the mouse 🖑 down and to the right until all the files in the group are selected.

SELECT ALL FILES

1 Open the folder containing the files.

2 Click **Edit**.

3 Click **Select All**.

Note: A quick way to select all the files in a folder is to press Ctrl + A .

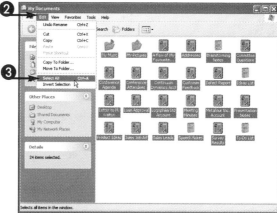

 TIP

How do I deselect a file?

To deselect a single file from a multiple-file selection, hold down Ctrl and click the file you want to deselect.

To deselect all files, click an empty area within the folder.

To reverse the selection — deselect the selected files and select the deselected files — click **Edit**, and then click **Invert Selection**.

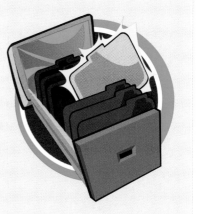

You can make an exact copy of a file, which is useful if you want to make a backup of an important file on a floppy disk or other removable disk, or if you want to send the copy on a disk to another person.

This section shows you how to copy a single file, but the steps also work if you select multiple files. You can also use these steps to copy a folder.

Copy a File

1 Open the folder containing the file you want to copy.

2 Select the file.

3 Click **Edit**.

4 Click **Copy To Folder**.

The Copy Items dialog box appears.

5 Click the location you want to use to store the copy.

Note: If the folder you want to use to store the copy is inside one of the displayed disk drives or folders, click 田 *to display the location's folder, and then click the folder you want.*

6 Click **Copy**.

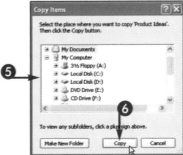

When you need to store a file in a new location, the easiest way is to move the file from its current folder to another folder on your computer.

This task shows you how to move a single file, but the steps also work if you select multiple files. You can also use these steps to move a folder.

Move a File

1. Open the folder containing the file you want to move.
2. Select the file.
3. Click **Edit**.
4. Click **Move To Folder**.

The Move Items dialog box appears.

5. Click the new location you want to use for the file.

Note: If the folder you want to use for the new location is inside one of the displayed disk drives or folders, click ⊞ to display the location's folder, and then click the folder you want.

6. Click **Move**.

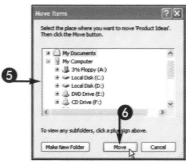

If your computer has a recordable CD drive, you can copy files and folders to a recordable CD. This enables you to store a large amount of data in a single place for convenient transport, storage, or backup.

If you want to copy music files to a CD, see the section "Burn Music Files to a CD" in Chapter 5.

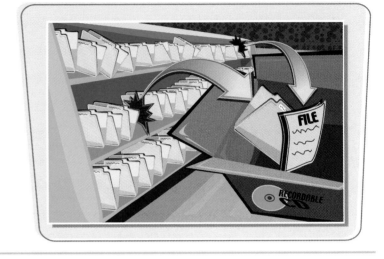

Copy Files to a CD

① Insert a recordable CD into your recordable CD drive.

A dialog box may appear asking what you want Windows to do with the disc.

② Click **Take No Action**.

③ Click **OK**.

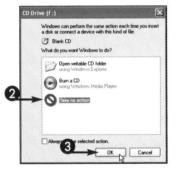

④ Select the files you want to copy to the CD.

⑤ Click **Edit**.

⑥ Click **Copy To Folder**.

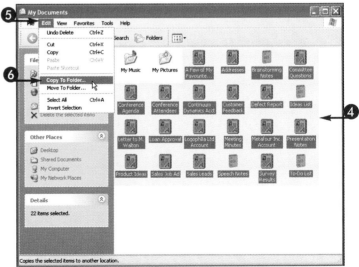

The Copy Items dialog box appears.

7 Click the drive that corresponds to your recordable CD drive.

8 Click **Copy**.

Windows XP places the selected files in a temporary storage area.

Note: *Repeat steps 4 to 8 for any other files or folders that you want to copy to the CD.*

9 Click **start**.

10 Click **My Computer**.

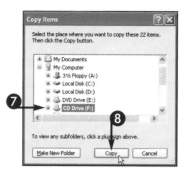

continued

 TIPS

Are there different types of recordable CDs I can use?

Recordable CDs come in two formats. The CD-R (recordable) format enables you to copy files to the disc only once. After the initial copy operation, the disc is locked and you cannot copy more files to it. Also, you cannot delete files from a CD-R disc.

The CD-RW (rewritable) format enables you to copy files to the disc multiple times as well as delete files from the disc.

How much data can I store on a recordable CD?

Most recordable CDs can hold about 650 MB (megabytes) of information. If a typical word processing document is about 50 KB (kilobytes), this means you can store about 13,000 files on a recordable CD. For larger files, such as images, you can store about 650 1 MB files on the disc.

Although Windows XP displays a Copying dialog box after you click the Copy button, the files are not yet copied to the CD. Instead, Windows copies the files to a temporary storage location on your hard drive. This enables you to copy files from different locations and to delete files before committing them to the CD.

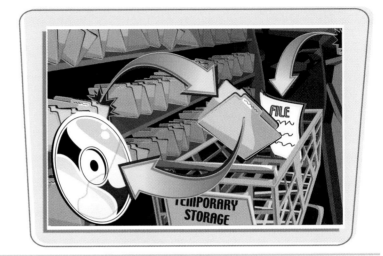

Copy Files to a CD *(continued)*

The My Computer window appears.

⑪ Double-click the icon for your computer's recordable CD drive.

The CD drive window opens and shows the files that are ready to be copied to the CD.

⑫ Click **File**.

⑬ Click **Write these files to CD**.

The CD Writing Wizard appears.

⑭ Type the name you want to use for the CD.

⑮ Click **Next**.

The wizard copies the files to the CD.

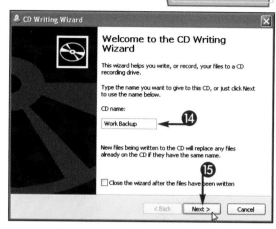

The final CD Writing Wizard dialog box appears.

Windows XP ejects the CD from the drive.

⑯ Click **Finish**.

Note: To view the files on the CD, insert the disc, open the My Computer window, and then double-click the icon for the recordable CD drive.

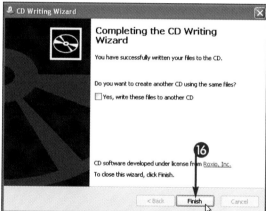

TIPS

How can I tell how much data I am copying to the CD?

❶ Open the recordable CD drive's window.

❷ Select all the files in the section named **Files Ready to Be Written to the CD**.

❸ Click **File**.

❹ Click **Properties**.

The Properties dialog box appears.

❺ Read the **Size on disk** number.

I want to start over with a CD-RW disc. Is there an easy way to erase the disc?

❶ Open the recordable CD drive's window.

❷ Click **File**.

❸ Click **Erase this CD-RW**.

The CD Writing Wizard appears.

❹ Click **Next**.

❺ Click **Finish**.

Rename a File

You can change the names of your files, which is useful if the current name of the file does not accurately describe the contents of the file. By giving your documents descriptive names, you make it easier to later find the file you want.

Make sure that you only rename those documents that you have created yourself or that have been given to you by someone else. Do not rename any of the Windows XP system files or any files associated with your programs, or your computer may behave erratically or crash.

Rename a File

① Open the folder that contains the file you want to rename.

② Click the file to select it.

Note: *In addition to renaming files, you can also rename any folders that you created yourself.*

③ Click **File**.

④ Click **Rename**.

A text box appears around the file name.

Note: *You can also select the Rename command by pressing* F2 *.*

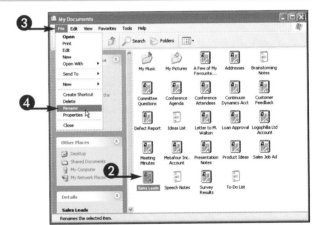

⑤ Type the new name you want to use for the file.

Note: *If you decide that you do not want to rename the file after all, press* Esc *to cancel the operation.*

Note: *The name you type can be up to 255 characters long, but it cannot include the following characters:* < >, ? : " \ *.

⑥ Press Enter or click an empty section of the folder.

The new name appears under the file's icon.

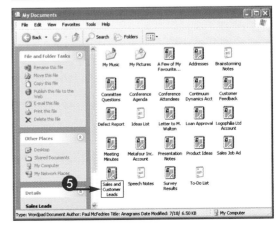

You can quickly create a new file directly within a file folder. This method is faster and often more convenient than running a program's New command, as explained in the section "Create a Document" in Chapter 3.

Create a New File

① Open the folder in which you want to create the file.

② Click **File**.

③ Click **New**.

④ Click the type of file you want to create.

Note: *If you click **Folder**, Windows XP creates a new subfolder.*

Note: *The New menu on your system may contain more items than you see here because some programs install their own file types.*

An icon for the new file appears in the folder.

⑤ Type the name you want to use for the new file.

⑥ Press **Enter**.

When you have a file that you no longer need, rather than leaving the file to clutter your hard drive, you can delete it.

Make sure that you only delete those documents that you have created yourself or that have been given to you by someone else. Do not delete any of the Windows XP system files or any files associated with your programs, or your computer may behave erratically or crash.

Delete a File

① Open the folder that contains the file you want to delete.

② Click the file you want to delete.

Note: *If you need to remove more than one file, select all the files you want to delete.*

③ Click **File**.

④ Click **Delete**.

Note: *Another way to select the **Delete** command is to press the* Delete *key.*

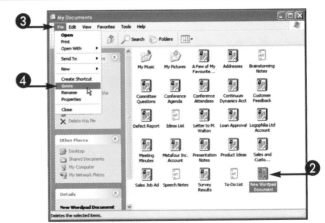

● The Confirm File Delete dialog box appears.

⑤ Click **Yes**.

The file disappears from the folder.

Note: *Another way to delete a file is to click and drag it to the desktop's Recycle Bin icon.*

If you delete a file in error,
Windows XP enables you to
restore the file by placing it back
in the folder from which you
deleted it.

**You can restore a deleted file because
Windows XP stores each deleted file in a
special folder called the Recycle Bin, where
the file stays for a few days or a few weeks,
depending on how often you empty the bin
or how full the folder becomes.**

Restore a Deleted File

① Double-click **Recycle Bin**.

The Recycle Bin window appears.

② Click the file you want to restore.

③ Click **File**.

④ Click **Restore**.

The file disappears from the Recycle Bin and
reappears in its original folder.

After you have used your computer for a while and you have created many documents, you might have trouble locating a specific file. You can save a great deal of time by having Windows XP search for your document.

Search for a File

① Click **start**.

② Click **Search**.

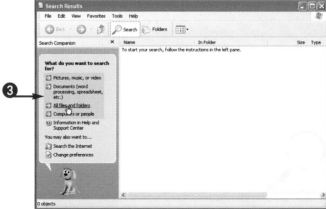

The Search Results window appears with the Search Companion on the left side of the window.

*Note: If you have My Documents or another folder window open, another way to display the Search Companion is to click the **Search** toolbar icon.*

③ Click the type of file you want to search for.

*Note: The most common choice is **All files and folders**, and the rest of the steps in this section assume you click this option.*

● The Search Companion displays controls so you can specify your search criteria.

④ To search according to file name, type part of or the entire file name.

⑤ To search according to file contents, type a word or phrase.

⑥ Click 🔽 and choose a location in which to search for the file.

⑦ Click **Search**.

● A list of files that match your search criteria appears.

● To open the folder than contains the file you want, click **File**, and then click **Open Containing Folder**.

Note: *To open just the file, double-click it.*

⑧ When you are done, click **Close** (☒) to close the Search Results window.

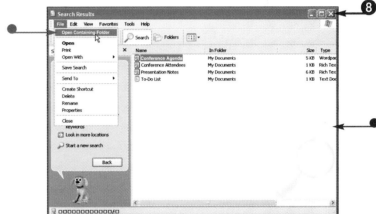

I know when I last worked on the file I am looking for. Can I use that information to find the file?

❶ In the Search Companion, scroll down and click **When was it modified?**.

❷ Click the time that corresponds to when you last worked on the file (○ changes to ◉).

❸ If you clicked **Specify dates**, click 🔽 in each of the lists to specify the range of dates in which you want to search.

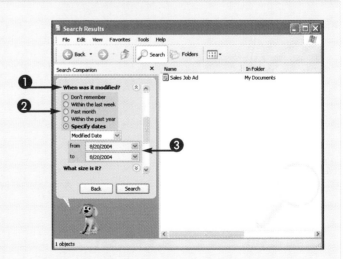

Extract Files from a Compressed Folder

If someone sends you a file via e-mail, or if you download a file from the Internet, the file often arrives in *compressed* form, which means the file actually contains one or more files that have been compressed to save space. To use the files on your computer, you need to extract them from the compressed file.

Because a compressed file can contain one or more files, it acts like a kind of folder. Therefore, Windows XP calls such files *compressed folders, zipped folders*, or *ZIP archives*.

Extract Files from a Compressed Folder

① Open the folder containing the compressed folder.

② Click the compressed folder.

③ Click **File**.

④ Click **Extract All**.

Note: You may not see the Extract All command if you have installed some other compression program such as WinZip.

The Extraction Wizard appears.

⑤ Click **Next**.

The Select a Destination screen of the Extraction Wizard appears.

6 Browse to or type the location of the folder into which you want the files extracted.

7 Click **Next**.

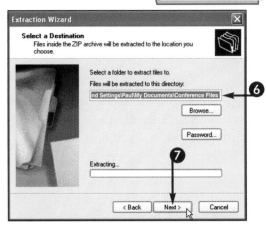

The Extraction Complete screen of the Extraction Wizard appears.

8 If you want to open the folder into which you extracted the files, click **Show extracted files** (☐ changes to ☑).

9 Click **Finish**.

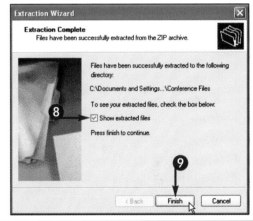

TIPS

How can I create a compressed folder?

1 Select the files and folders you want to store in the compressed folder.

2 Click **File**.

3 Click **Send To**.

4 Click **Compressed (zipped) Folder**.

The compressed folder appears.

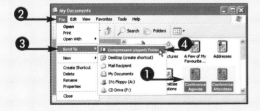

Can I password-protect a compressed folder?

Yes, you can add a password to the folder, and only a person who knows the password can extract the files. Double-click the compressed folder to open it and then click **File, Add a Password**. Type your password in the Password and Confirm Password text boxes, and then click **OK**.

Sharing Your Computer with Others

If you share your computer with other people, you can create separate user accounts so that each person works only with his/her own documents, programs, and Windows XP settings. This chapter shows you how to create and change user accounts, how to log on and off different accounts, and how to share documents between accounts.

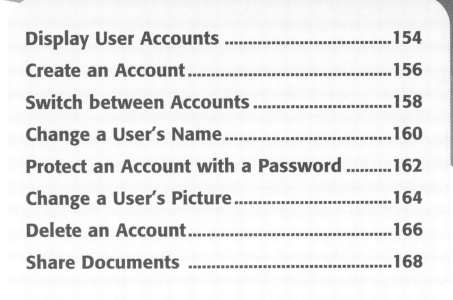

Display User Accounts

To create, change, or delete user accounts, you need to display the User Accounts window.

① Click **start**.

② Click **Control Panel**.

The Control Panel window appears.

③ Click **User Accounts**.

The User Accounts window appears.

● These icons represent the existing user accounts.

Note: *If you did not install Windows XP yourself, the computer administrator account is called Owner.*

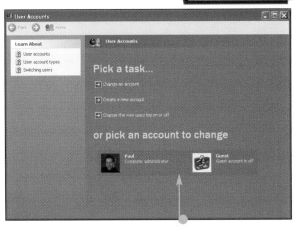

● The computer administrator account is created when you install Windows XP. When you start Windows XP, you log on with this account.

● The Guest account is a limited account that enables a person who does not have an account to use the computer. To turn on the Guest account, click **Guest**, and then click **Turn On the Guest Account**.

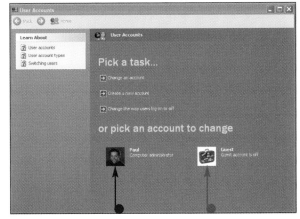

TIP

How do user accounts help me share my computer with other people?

Without user accounts, anyone who uses your computer can view and even change your documents, Windows XP settings, e-mail accounts and messages, Internet Explorer favorites, and more.

With user accounts, users get their own My Documents folder, personalized Windows XP settings, e-mail accounts, and favorites. In short, users get their own version of Windows XP to personalize without interfering with anyone else's.

Create an Account

If you want to share your computer with another person, then you can create a user account for that individual.

Note that you must be logged on to Windows XP with an administrator account to create a user account.

Create an Account

① Display the User Accounts window.

Note: See the section "Display User Accounts" for more information.

② Click **Create a new account**.

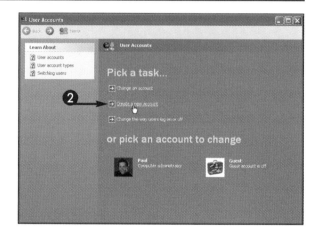

③ Type the name you want to use for the new account.

④ Click **Next**.

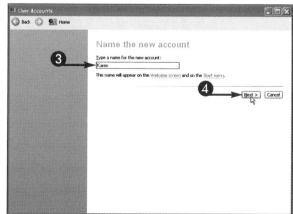

5 Click the account type you want (⃝ changes to ⦿).

6 Click **Create Account**.

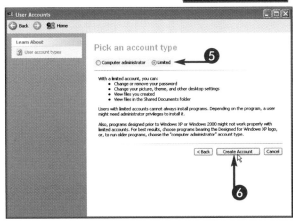

● The new account appears in the User Accounts window.

TIP

How do I decide what type of account to give each user?

The two different account types — Computer administrator and Limited — affect the extent to which the user can interact with the computer:

● A *computer administrator* has complete access to the computer, including access to all users' documents. Administrators can also install programs and devices and add, change, and delete user accounts.

● A *limited user* has partial access to the computer. These users can access only their own documents, as well as any documents that other users have designated to share. Limited users can modify only their own settings, and can change some aspects of their user account, including their password and picture.

Switch between Accounts

After you have created more than one account on your computer, you can switch between accounts. This is useful when one person is already working in Windows XP and another person needs to use the computer.

Windows XP leaves the original user's programs and windows running so that after the second person is finished, the original user can log on again and continue working as before.

Switch between Accounts

① Click **start**.

② Click **Log Off**.

The Log Off Windows dialog box appears.

③ Click **Switch User**.

The Welcome screen appears.

④ Click the name of the user account you want to switch to.

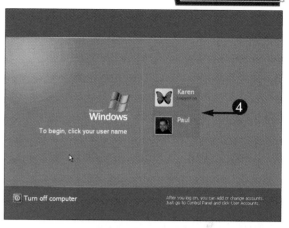

● If the account is protected by a password, the password box appears.

Note: See the section "Protect an Account with a Password" in this chapter for details on protecting an account with a password.

⑤ Type the password.

Note: If you cannot remember your password, click ? to display a password hint.

⑥ Click →.

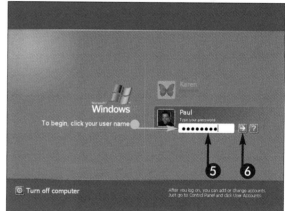

 TIP

When I click Log Off, Windows XP takes me directly to the Welcome screen and does not keep my programs running. How can I fix this?

Your version of Windows XP is not set up for *Fast User Switching*. You can fix this by following these steps:

① In the User Accounts window, click **Change the way users log on or off**.

Note: See the section "Display User Accounts" to access this window.

② Click **Use Fast User Switching** (☐ changes to ☑).

③ Click **Apply Options**.

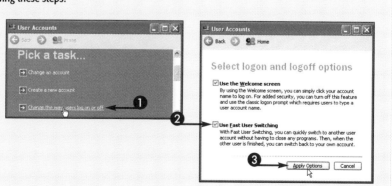

Change a User's Name

If the name you are using now is not suitable for some reason, you can change it to a different name.

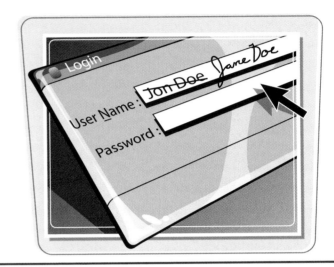

Change a User's Name

1 Display the User Accounts window.

Note: See the section "Display User Accounts" to access this window.

2 Click the user account you want to work with.

3 Click **Change the name**.

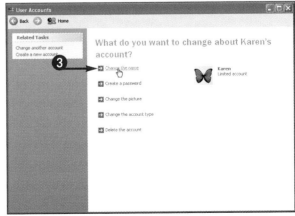

④ Type the new name.

⑤ Click **Change Name**.

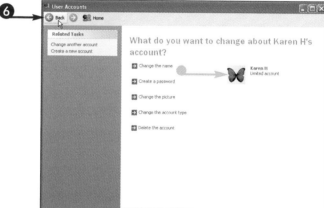

● The new name appears in the user's window.

⑥ Click **Back** to return to the User Accounts window.

Are there any restrictions in the names I can use?
Yes, you have to watch out for the following:

● The name cannot be any longer than 20 characters.

● The name cannot include any of the following characters:
, < > / ? ; : " [ ] \ | = + *

● The name cannot be the same as the computer's name. To check the computer name, click **start**, right-click **My Computer**, click **Properties**, and then click the **Computer Name** tab. This tab displays the computer name.

Protect an Account with a Password

You can protect your account with a password. This is often a good idea because otherwise another user can log on to your account just by clicking your user name in the Welcome screen.

① Display the User Accounts window.

Note: See the section "Display User Accounts" to access this window.

② Click the user account you want to work with.

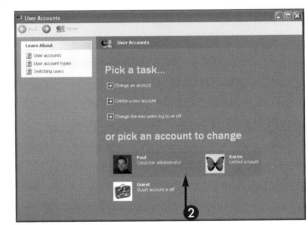

③ Click **Create a password**.

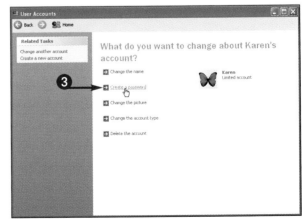

④ Type the password.

⑤ Type the password again.

⑥ Type a word or phrase to use as a password hint in case you forget the password.

⑦ Click **Create Password**.

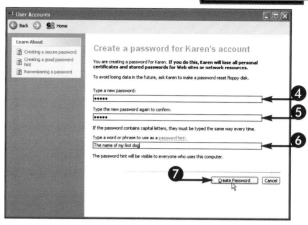

● The user's window appears and indicates that the account is now password protected.

⑧ Click **Back** to return to the User Accounts window.

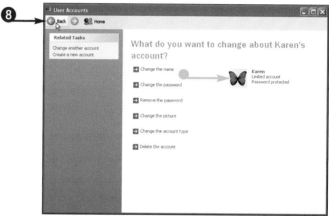

TIPS

How do I change the password?

① Click the user account you want to work with.

② Click **Change the password**.

③ Type the password.

④ Type the password again.

⑤ Type a word or phrase to use as a password hint in case you forget the password.

⑥ Click **Change Password**.

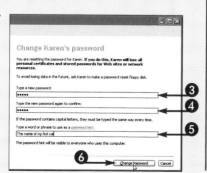

How do I remove the password?

① Click the user account you want to work with.

② Click **Remove the password**.

③ Read the details and click **Remove Password**.

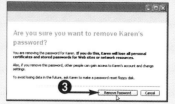

Change a User's Picture

Windows XP assigns a random picture to each new user account, and this picture appears in the User Accounts window, the Welcome screen, and the Start menu. If you do not like your picture, or if you have a more suitable picture that you would prefer to use, you can change your picture.

Change a User's Picture

1 Display the User Accounts window.

Note: See the section "Display User Accounts" to access this window.

2 Click the user account you want to work with.

3 Click **Change the picture**.

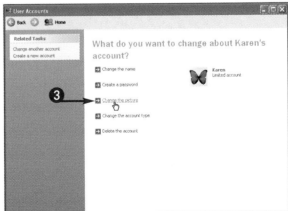

④ Click the picture you want to use.

⑤ Click **Change Picture**.

● The user's window appears and displays the new picture.

⑥ Click **Back** to return to the User Accounts window.

TIP

How do I use one of my own pictures?

① Click the user account you want to work with.

② Click **Change the picture**.

③ Click **Browse for more pictures**.

The Open dialog box appears.

④ Open the folder containing the picture you want to use and then click the picture.

⑤ Click **Open**.

⑥ Click **Change Picture**.

Delete an
Account

You can delete a user's account
when it is no longer needed.
This reduces the number of
users on the User Accounts and
Welcome screens and possibly
frees up some disk space.

Delete an Account

① Display the User Accounts window.

Note: *See the section "Display User Accounts" to access this window.*

② Click the user account you want to delete.

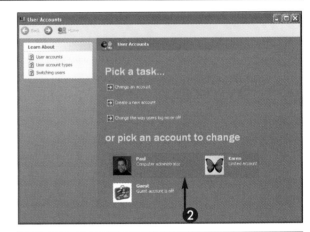

③ Click **Delete the account**.

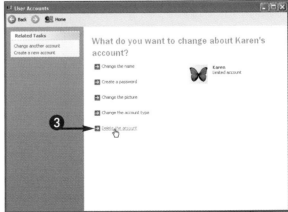

④ Click a button to specify whether you want to keep or delete the user's personal files.

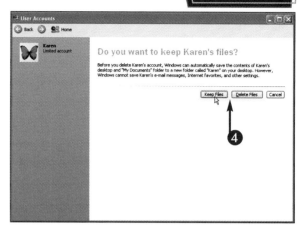

⑤ Click **Delete Account**.

Windows XP deletes the account.

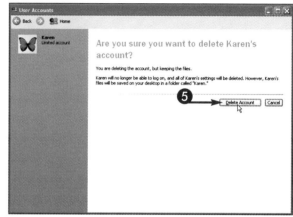

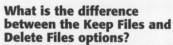

TIPS

My user account does not offer the Delete the account task. Why not?

If yours is the only computer administrator account left on the computer, Windows XP will not allow you to delete it. Windows XP requires that there always be at least one computer administrator account on the computer.

What is the difference between the Keep Files and Delete Files options?

● Click **Keep Files** to retain the user's personal files — the contents of his or her My Documents folder and desktop. These files are saved on your desktop in a folder named after the user. All other personal items — settings, e-mail accounts and messages, and Internet Explorer favorites — are deleted.

● Click **Delete Files** to delete all of the user's personal files, settings, messages, and favorites.

Share Documents

You can share documents of your choice with the other users set up on your computer.

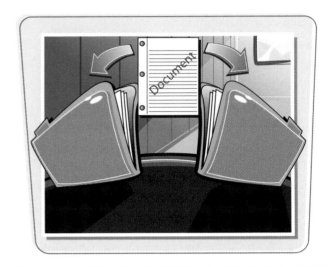

Share Documents

SHARE A DOCUMENT

1 Open the folder containing the document you want to share.

2 Click the document.

Note: If you want to share more than one document, select all the documents you want to share.

3 Click **Edit**.

4 Click **Copy To Folder**.

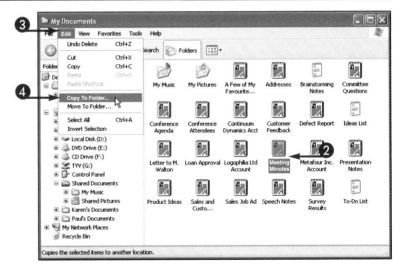

The Copy Items dialog box appears.

5 Click **Shared Documents**.

6 Click **Copy**.

Windows XP makes copies of the documents in the Shared Documents folder.

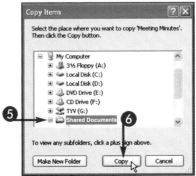

VIEW SHARED DOCUMENTS

1 Click **start**.

2 Click **My Computer**.

The My Computer window appears.

3 Double-click **Shared Documents**.

The Shared Documents window appears.

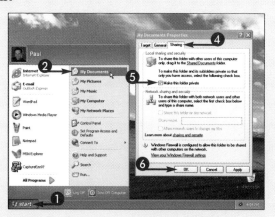

TIP

Other computer administrators can view my My Documents folder. How can I protect My Documents?

You can make My Documents private by following these steps:

1 Click **start**.

2 Right-click **My Documents**.

3 Click **Properties**.

The My Documents Properties dialog box opens.

4 Click the **Sharing** tab.

5 Click **Make this folder private** (☐ changes to ☑).

6 Click **OK**.

Using Windows XP's Notebook Features

Windows XP comes with many features designed specifically for notebook computers. In this chapter you learn how to monitor battery life, specify a scheme for saving power, synchronize files between a notebook and a desktop PC, and more.

Display Power Options

You can get the most out of your notebook battery by monitoring the battery level and by shutting down components when you are not using them. Windows XP's Power Options dialog box is the source for these and other notebook operations.

1 Click **start**.

2 Click **Control Panel**.

The Control Panel window appears.

3 Click **Printers and Other Hardware**.

The Printers and Other Hardware window appears.

④ Click **Power Options**.

The Power Options Properties dialog box appears.

⑤ Click the **Power Meter** tab.

The current battery level appears.

● This version of the Power Meter icon appears when your notebook is running on AC power.

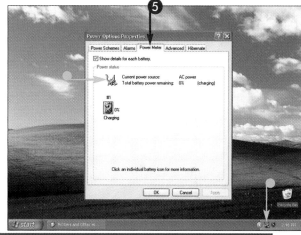

TIPS

Is there a quicker way to monitor my notebook battery level?

Yes. The taskbar's notification area includes a Power Meter icon. When the battery is at maximum charge, the icon shows as all blue. As the battery charge falls, the amount of blue in the icon also falls. Note, too, that when you position your mouse pointer (⤷) over the icon, a banner pops up to show you the current battery level.

● The Power Meter icon

Is there a quicker way to open the Power Options dialog box?

Yes. Follow these steps:

① Right-click the Power Meter icon in the taskbar's notification area.

② Click **Adjust Power Properties**.

Set Battery Alarms

When you use your notebook on battery power, you can avoid having the power shut down while you are working by setting alarms that warn you when the battery charge is getting low.

You can set two alarm levels. The Low Battery Alarm warns you when the battery charge is getting low; the Critical Battery Alarm warns you when the battery charge is getting dangerously low and you need to take immediate action.

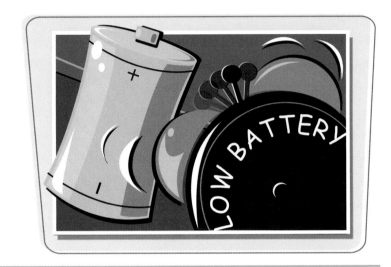

Set Battery Alarms

① Display the Power Options Properties dialog box.

② Click the **Alarms** tab.

③ Click and drag the slider to set the low battery alarm level.

④ Click **Alarm Action**.

The Low Battery Alarm Actions dialog box appears. You can set up actions for Windows XP to take when your notebook reaches the low battery level here.

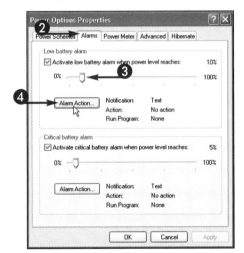

⑤ To sound an alarm, click **Sound alarm** (☐ changes to ☑).

⑥ If you do not want Windows XP to display a dialog box, click **Display message** (☑ changes to ☐).

⑦ To specify an action, click here (☐ changes to ☑).

⑧ Click ☑ and choose an action from the list.

⑨ Click **OK**.

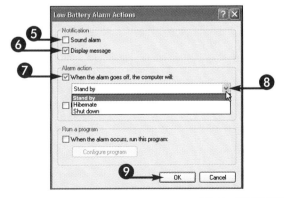

⑩ Click and drag the slider to set the critical battery alarm level.

⑪ Click **Alarm Action**.

The Critical Battery Alarm Actions dialog box appears. You can set up actions that Windows XP takes when your notebook reaches critical battery level here.

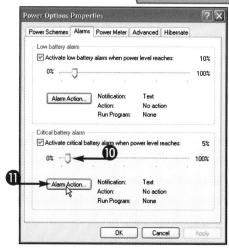

⑫ To sound an alarm, click **Sound alarm** (☐ changes to ☑).

⑬ If you do not want Windows XP to display a dialog box, click **Display message** (☑ changes to ☐).

⑭ To specify an action, click here (☐ changes to ☑).

⑮ Click ▾ and choose an action from the list.

⑯ Click **OK**.

What is the difference between the Stand by, Hibernate, and Shut down actions?

Stand by shuts off a notebook's screen and hard drive, saving battery power. Use this option if you have an AC outlet nearby.

Hibernate shuts down the computer to save power, but remembers all of your open windows and documents, restoring them when you restart. Use this option if do not have an AC outlet handy but you want to preserve your work. Remembering your open windows and documents takes time, so this option is not the best choice for the Critical Battery Alarm. If you do not see this option in the Power Options Properties dialog box, click the **Hibernate** tab, click **Enable Hibernation** (○ changes to ◉), and then click **Apply**.

Shut down saves power by shutting down the computer. Use this action when you have no AC outlet nearby and you need to shut down as quickly as possible.

Specify a
Power Scheme

You can preserve battery power by setting up a *power scheme* that turns off the monitor, hard drive, or the entire computer after you have not used the machine for a while.

A power scheme is useful because even when your notebook is sitting idle, it is still using the battery to power the monitor and the constantly spinning hard drive.

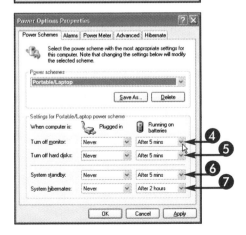

Specify a Power Scheme

① Display the Power Options Properties dialog box.

② Click the **Power Schemes** tab.

③ Click ⊡ to select a predefined power scheme.

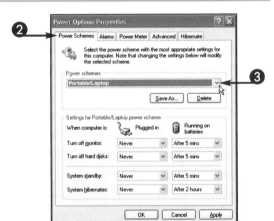

④ Click ⊡ to specify the number of minutes or hours of idle time after which the notebook monitor turns off.

⑤ Click ⊡ to specify the number of minutes or hours of idle time after which the notebook hard disks turn off.

⑥ Click ⊡ to specify the number of minutes or hours of idle time after which the computer goes into standby mode.

⑦ Click ⊡ to specify the number of minutes or hours of idle time after which the computer goes into hibernate mode.

Configure Power Buttons

You can configure your notebook's power buttons to perform actions, such as going into standby mode or hibernating. This gives you a quick way to initiate these actions.

There are three power "buttons" on most notebooks: The on/off (power) button, the sleep button, and closing the lid. If your notebook does not have a sleep button, you can usually simulate one by tapping the on/off button quickly.

Configure Power Buttons

① Display the Power Options Properties dialog box.

② Click the **Advanced** tab.

③ Click ⬇ and click the action to perform when you close the notebook's lid.

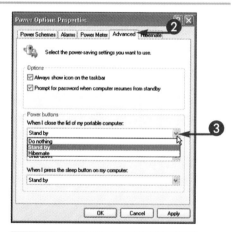

④ Click ⬇ and click the action to perform when you press the notebook's on/off (power) button.

⑤ Click ⬇ and click the action to perform when you press the notebook's sleep button.

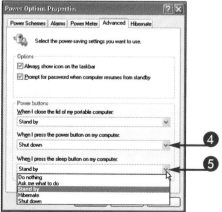

Synchronize Files between Computers

If you use both a notebook computer and a desktop computer, you may often have to use the same files on both computers. To avoid having multiple versions of a file or losing work by accidentally copying over a file, Windows XP enables you to synchronize files between the two computers.

The file synchronization is handled automatically when you use a special folder called a Briefcase.

Add Files to a Briefcase

CREATE A BRIEFCASE

1 On the computer that contains the original files you want to work with, insert the disk you want to use to transfer the files.

Note: You can use a floppy disk, ZIP disk, or other removable disk. Remember that you must have the same type of disk drive on both computers.

2 Click **start**.

3 Click **My Computer**.

The My Computer window opens.

4 Double-click the disk drive that contains the removable disk you inserted in step **1**.

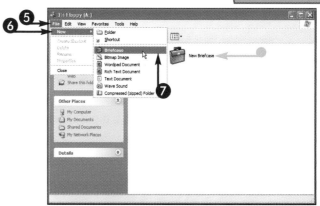

The removable disk's window appears.

⑤ Click **File**.

⑥ Click **New**.

⑦ Click **Briefcase**.

● A new Briefcase folder appears on the removable disk.

TRANSFER FILES TO THE BRIEFCASE

① Click **start**.

② Click **My Documents**.

TIPS

Do I have to create a new Briefcase each time I want to transfer files between computers?

No, you can use the same Briefcase for many different transfers. This is particularly handy if you transfer the same files repeatedly. You can leave those files in the Briefcase and just update them, as explained later in this section.

Are there any circumstances where I would need more than one Briefcase?

Yes. Many people create separate Briefcase folders for things like projects, departments, and customers, as well as to keep personal files separate from business files. If you do this, it is important to rename each new Briefcase folder to something meaningful so that you can easily differentiate between them.

continued

After you transfer the files from the Briefcase to the other computer, you can work on the files just like any other document.

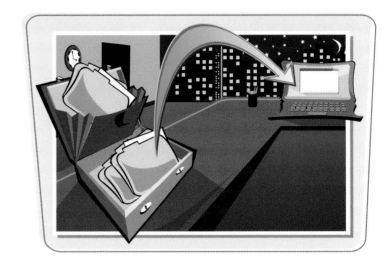

Add Files to a Briefcase *(continued)*

The My Documents window opens.

Note: *If the files you want to work with on the other computer are located in a subfolder of My Documents, open that subfolder.*

③ Click and drag the files from My Documents to the Briefcase folder on the removable disk.

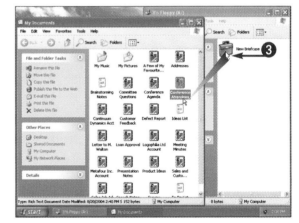

WORK WITH THE FILES ON THE OTHER COMPUTER

① Eject the removable disk and insert it into the other computer.

② On the other computer, click **start**.

③ Click **My Computer**.

The My Computer window opens.

4 Double-click the disk drive that contains the removable disk you inserted in step **1**.

The removable disk's window appears.

5 Double-click the Briefcase folder.

The files in the Briefcase appear.

Note: *The first time you open a Briefcase folder, a welcome message appears. Click **Finish** to close this message.*

6 Copy the files from the Briefcase to the other computer's My Documents folder.

7 Open and work with the files as needed.

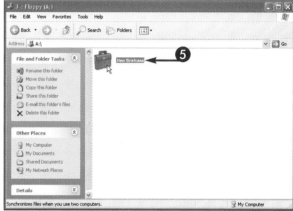

TIPS

Can I work with files directly from the Briefcase?

Yes. When you work with the files directly, you do not need to update the Briefcase. After you have finished working with the files, eject the disk, insert it into the original computer, and then update the files. However, working with the files directly from the Briefcase is usually slower because most removable drives have slower response times than a hard drive.

What happens if I create a new document on the other computer?

When you copy the new document to the Briefcase folder and insert the disk into the original computer, Windows XP treats the new file as an "orphan" because it does not know where the file is supposed to be stored on the original computer. Copying the file to My Documents synchronizes the original computer and the Briefcase.

continued

Synchronize Files between Computers *(continued)*

You can synchronize the files after you have finished working with them. You first update the Briefcase with any changes you made on the other computer, and then you update the file on the original computer.

SYCHRONIZE THE FILES ON THE OTHER COMPUTER

① Open the Briefcase folder on the removable disk in the other computer.

② Click **Briefcase**.

③ Click **Update All**.

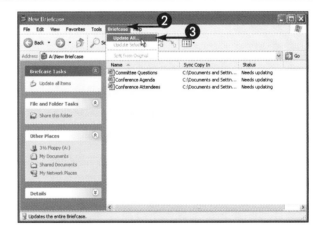

● Briefcase displays a list of files to be updated.

④ Click **Update**.

Briefcase updates the files on the removable disk with the changed files from the other computer.

⑤ Click ⊠ to close the Briefcase window.

SYCHRONIZE THE FILES ON THE ORIGINAL COMPUTER

① Eject the removable disk and insert it into the original computer.

② Open the Briefcase folder on the original computer.

③ Click **Briefcase**.

④ Click **Update All**.

● Briefcase displays a list of files to be updated.

⑤ Click **Update**.

Briefcase updates the files on the original computer with the changed files from the removable disk.

⑥ Click ⊠ to close the Briefcase window.

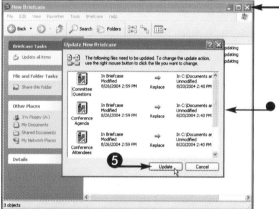

TIP

I transfer the same files repeatedly. Do I always have to copy those files from the original computer to the Briefcase?

No. Instead, you can simply update the Briefcase as follows:

① In the original computer, insert the disk containing the Briefcase folder.

② Use My Computer to open the Briefcase folder.

③ Click **Briefcase**.

④ Click **Update All**.

Briefcase displays a list of files to be updated.

⑤ Click **Update**.

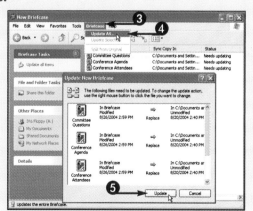

Insert a PC Card

You can use a PC Card (sometimes called a PCMCIA card), which is a credit card–sized device that plugs into a special socket on your notebook, to expand your notebook's capabilities.

PC Cards support many different types of devices, including modems, network adapters, hard drives, and more.

Insert a PC Card

① Insert the PC Card device into an empty PC Card socket on your notebook computer.

A beep is heard on your computer speaker.

Note: *If you have not inserted the PC Card before, the Found New Hardware Wizard appears.*

② Insert the floppy disk or CD that came with the device.

③ Click **Next**.

Windows XP installs the software for the device.

Note: *If Windows XP warns you that the device has not passed Windows Logo testing, click* ***Continue Anyway***.

When the installation is complete, the final wizard dialog box appears.

④ Click **Finish**.

● The Safely Remove Hardware icon () appears in the notification area.

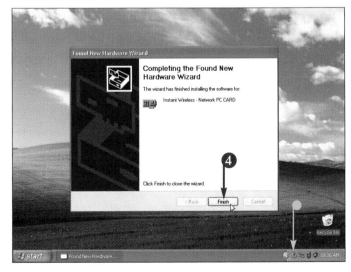

When you no longer need a PC Card device, you should remove it from your notebook computer.

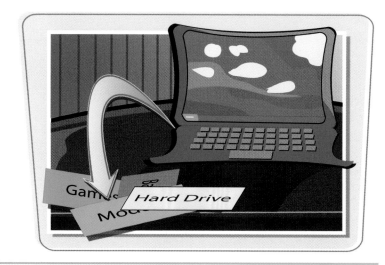

However, problems can arise if you do not allow Windows XP to shut down the device properly.

Remove a PC Card

① Click ▣ in the taskbar's notification area.

A list of the devices that are attached to your notebook computer appears.

② Click the device you want to remove.

Windows XP displays a message telling you that it is okay to remove the device.

③ Remove the device from the PC Card socket.

CHAPTER 9

Getting Connected to the Internet

The Internet is a vast, worldwide network that enables you to read World Wide Web pages, send an e-mail message, and puts a vast world of information at your fingertips. This chapter shows you how to get your computer connected to the Internet.

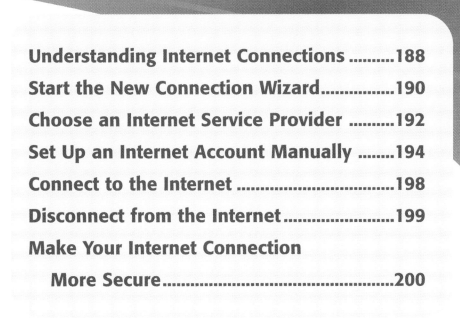

Understanding Internet Connections

Before you connect to the Internet, you need to know how to set up your modem, and you need to know how to choose an Internet service provider.

Serial Cable

Run this cable from the modem to the serial port in the back of your computer. You do not need to do this if your modem resides inside your computer's case.

Phone Line

Run one phone cable from the wall jack to the jack labeled *Line* in the back of the modem. This jack may also be labeled *Telco* or it may just show a picture of a wall jack.

Telephone Connection

Run a second phone cable from the telephone to the jack labeled *Phone* on the back of the modem. This jack may also just show a picture of a telephone.

Internet Service Provider

An *Internet service provider* (ISP) supplies you with an account that enables you to access the Internet. You dial up the ISP using your computer's modem, and then the ISP connects your computer to the Internet.

Connection Charges

The ISP charges you a monthly fee, which can range from a few dollars a month to $40 or $50 dollars a month, depending on the connection speed and how many minutes of connection time you are allowed each month. Note that most ISPs charge an extra fee per hour if you exceed your allotted time.

Connection Speed

Internet connections have different speeds, and this speed determines how fast the Internet data is sent to your computer. If you connect to your ISP using a modem, the connection speed may be as low as 28.8 kilobits per second, although most ISPs now support modem speeds of up to 56 kilobits per second. High-speed (or *broadband*) connections either via television cable or by ADSL phone lines offer speeds over 1,000 kilobits per second (or 1 megabit per second).

Start the New Connection Wizard

You can get help when trying to connect to the Internet from the New Connection Wizard, which takes you step-by-step through the process. This is much easier than trying to set up the connection on your own.

The New Connection Wizard gives you two ways to set up the connection: by choosing an ISP, or by setting up the connection manually. This section shows you how to start the wizard, and the next couple of sections take you through these two methods.

Start the New Connection Wizard

① Click **start**.

② Click **All Programs**.

③ Click **Accessories**.

④ Click **Communications**.

⑤ Click **New Connection Wizard**.

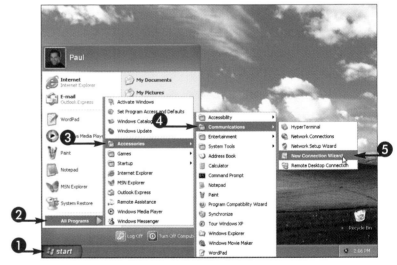

The New Connection Wizard appears.

⑥ Click **Next**.

The Network Connection Type dialog box appears.

7 Click **Connect to the Internet** (○ changes to ◉).

8 Click **Next**.

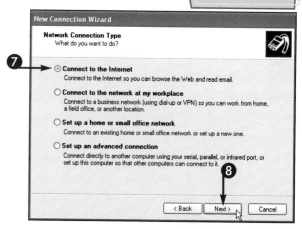

The Getting Ready dialog box appears.

9 Click the method you want to use to set up your Internet connection.

Note: *The next couple of sections take you through the specifics of the first two methods. For the third method, you do not need the wizard. Instead, insert the CD and follow the instructions that appear on the screen.*

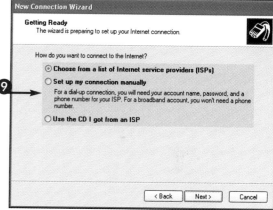

TIP

My computer is on a network and I want to connect to the Internet via one of the other computers. How do I do that?

1 Click **start**.

2 Click **All Programs**.

3 Click **Accessories**.

4 Click **Communications**.

5 Click **Network Setup Wizard**.

The Network Setup Wizard appears.

6 Click **Next**.

7 Click **Next**.

8 Click here (○ changes to ◉).

9 Click **Next** and follow the rest of the wizard's dialog boxes.

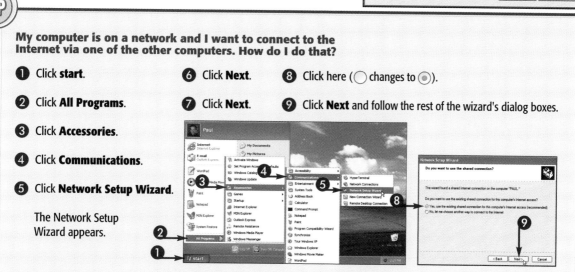

Choose an Internet Service Provider

If you do not have an account with an Internet service provider, the New Connection Wizard can offer you a list of ISPs in your area.

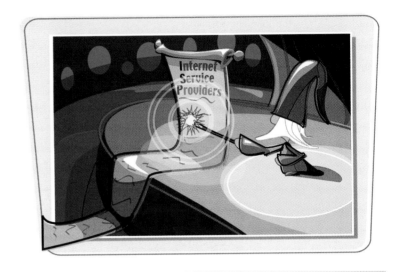

Choose an Internet Service Provider

1. In the New Connection Wizard's Getting Ready dialog box, click **Choose from a list of Internet service providers (ISPs)** (○ changes to ◉).

2. Click **Next**.

   The Completing the New Connection Wizard dialog box appears.

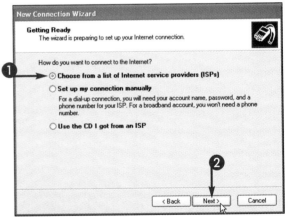

3. Click **Select from a list of other ISPs** (○ changes to ◉).

   Note: *If you prefer to use MSN as your ISP, click Get online with MSN, click Finish, and then follow the instructions that appear.*

4. Click **Finish**.

   Note: *If the Online Services window appears, double-click Refer me to more Internet service providers.*

   Note: *If the Phone and Modem Options dialog box appears, click New Location, and then click OK.*

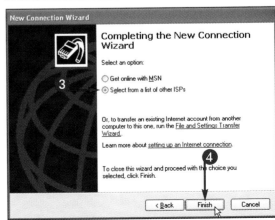

The Internet Connection Wizard loads and the Internet Sign-up Phone Numbers dialog box appears.

⑤ Click ▾ to choose your country or region.

⑥ Click **OK**.

The Internet Connection Wizard dials the Microsoft Internet Referral Service to get a list of ISPs in your area.

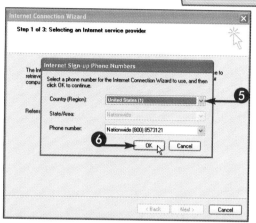

A list of ISPs in your area appears.

⑦ Click the ISP you want to sign up with.

● A description of the ISP appears.

⑧ Click **Next**.

⑨ Follow the instructions provided to sign up for the account.

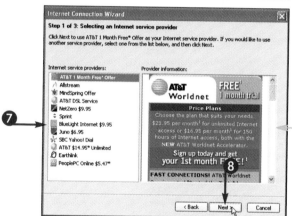

 TIP

Can I cancel an ISP account if I decide to sign up with a different ISP?

Yes. Most ISPs offer the ability to manage your account online using the ISPs home Web page. You can often cancel your account online, although most companies tend to make this option difficult to find. If you have trouble, for almost all ISPs you can cancel the account by contacting the Customer Service department.

If you have already established an account with an ISP, you can set up the account in Windows XP yourself by entering the data sent to you by your ISP.

1 In the New Connection Wizard's Getting Ready dialog box, click **Set up my account manually** (○ changes to ◉).

2 Click **Next**.

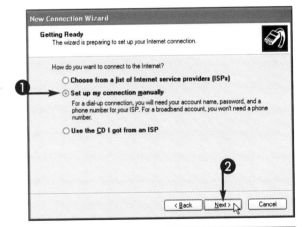

SET UP A DIAL-UP MODEM CONNECTION

The Internet Connection dialog box appears.

1 Click **Connect using a dial-up modem** (○ changes to ◉).

Note: *If your account is a broadband connection with a user name and password, click* **Connect using a broadband connection that requires a user name and password.** *You then follow the remaining steps, except you do not need to type a phone number.*

2 Click **Next**.

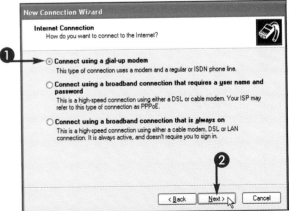

The Connection Name dialog box appears.

③ Type the name of your ISP.

④ Click **Next**.

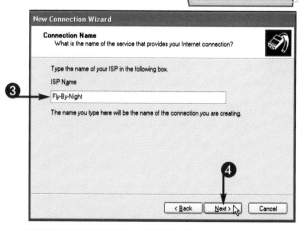

The Phone Number to Dial dialog box appears.

⑤ Type the phone number that your modem must dial to connect to the ISP.

Note: *Remember to include the area code if your area requires ten-digit dialing.*

⑥ Click **Next**.

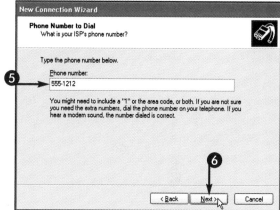

 TIPS

What information do I need to configure my dial-up account?

When you signed up for your account, the ISP you chose will have sent you the details you require to set up the account manually. There are three items you must have: your user name, your password, and the phone number your modem must dial to connect to the ISP.

My area requires 10-digit dialing. How do I handle this?

When you fill in the ISP's phone number, add the area code in front of the phone number. For example, if the area code is 317 and the phone number is 555-1212, type **317-555-1212**.

continued

With the New Connection Wizard, it is easy for you to set up an account manually. It takes you step-by-step through the information you need to specify.

The Internet Account Information dialog box appears.

⑦ Type the user name provided by your ISP.

⑧ Type your password.

● The password characters appear as dots for security.

Note: *If your password mixes uppercase and lowercase letters, type the letters using the exact case specified by your ISP.*

⑨ Type your password again.

⑩ Click **Next**.

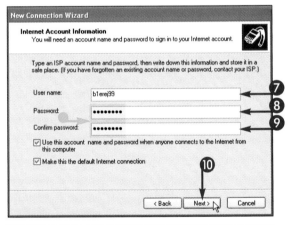

The Completing the New Connection Wizard dialog box appears.

⑪ If you want to add the connection to your desktop as a shortcut icon, click **Add a shortcut to this connection to my desktop** (☐ changes to ☑).

⑫ Click **Finish**.

SET UP A BROADBAND CONNECTION

① In the New Connection Wizard's Internet Connection dialog box, click **Connect using a broadband connection that is always on** (○ changes to ◉).

② Click **Next**.

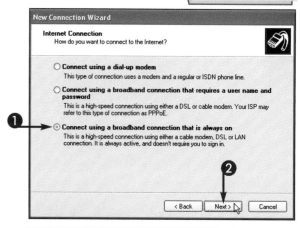

The Completing the New Connection Wizard dialog box appears.

③ Click **Finish**.

TIP

I have call waiting on my phone. Will that be a problem?

Yes, the call waiting beeps can disconnect your modem. To disable call waiting, follow these steps:

① Click **start**.

② Click **Control Panel**.

③ Click **Printers and Other Hardware**.

④ Click **Phone and Modem Options**.

⑤ Click **Edit**.

⑥ Click **To disable call waiting, dial** (☐ changes to ☑).

⑦ Click ☑, and then click the dialing sequence that disables call waiting in your area.

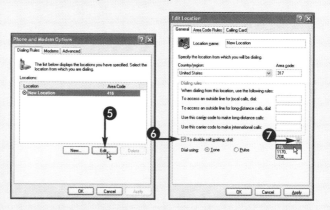

Connect to the Internet

Once you have your Internet account configured, you can use it to connect to the Internet.

Connect to the Internet

① Click **start**.

② Click **Connect To**.

*Note: If you do not see the Connect To command, click **Control Panel**, click **Network and Internet Connections**, click **Network Connections**, and then double-click your Internet connection.*

③ Click your Internet connection.

Note: If you elected to place a connection shortcut on your desktop, you can also double-click that icon.

● If your dial-up or broadband account requires a user name and password, the Connect dialog box appears.

④ Click **Dial**.

Windows XP connects to the Internet.

● When the connection is complete, this icon appears in the taskbar's notification area.

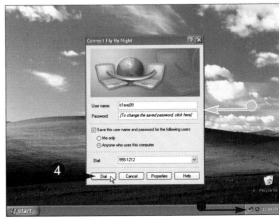

After you have completed your Internet session, you should disconnect to avoid running up your connection time unnecessarily.

Many ISPs give you only so much connection time per month, and they charge you a fee for each minute you go over your allotted time. Therefore, always disconnect when you are done to avoid running up your connection charges.

Disconnect from the Internet

1 Right-click the connection icon in the taskbar's notification area.

2 Click **Disconnect**.

Windows XP disconnects from the Internet.

Make Your Internet Connection More Secure

Because when your computer is connected to the Internet, it is possible for another person on the Internet to access your computer and infect it with a virus or cause other damage, you should turn on the Windows Firewall, which prevents intruders from accessing your computer while you are online.

The Security Center shown in this section comes with Windows XP Service Pack 2.

Make Your Internet Connection More Secure

① Click the Windows Security Alerts icon in the taskbar's notification area.

Note: *If you do not see the Windows Security Alerts icon, click* **start**, *click* **All Programs**, *click* **Accessories**, *click* **System Tools**, *and then click* **Security Center**.

The Security Center window appears.

② Check the **Firewall** setting.

③ If the **Firewall** setting reads **OFF**, click **Windows Firewall**.

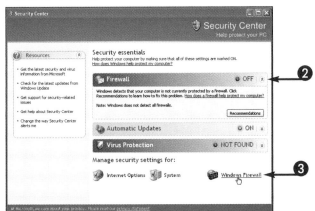

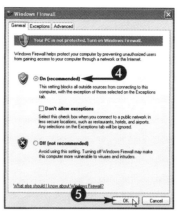

The Windows Firewall dialog box appears.

④ Click **On (recommended)** (○ changes to ⊙).

⑤ Click **OK**.

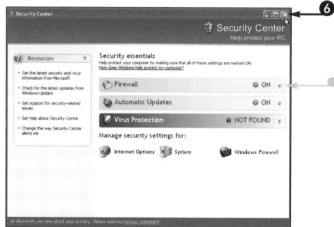

● In the Security Center window, the **Firewall** setting changes to **ON**.

⑥ Click 🗙 to close the Security Center window.

TIP

How do I activate the Windows Firewall if I do not have Service Pack 2?

① Click **start**.

② Click **Control Panel**.

③ Click **Network and Internet Connections**.

④ Click **Network Connections**.

⑤ Right-click your Internet connection and then click **Properties**.

⑥ Click the **Advanced** tab.

⑦ Click **Protect my computer and network by limiting or preventing access to this computer from the Internet** (☐ changes to ☑).

⑧ Click **OK**.

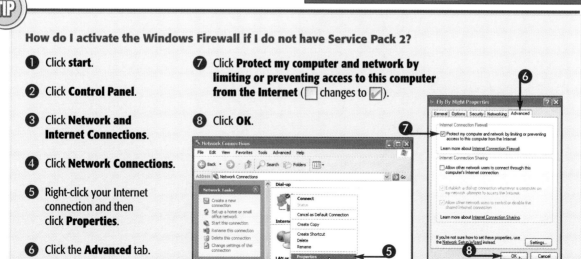

Surfing the World Wide Web

After you have your Internet connection up and running, you can use Windows XP's Internet Explorer program to navigate — or surf — the sites of the World Wide Web. This chapter explains the Web and shows you how to navigate from site to site.

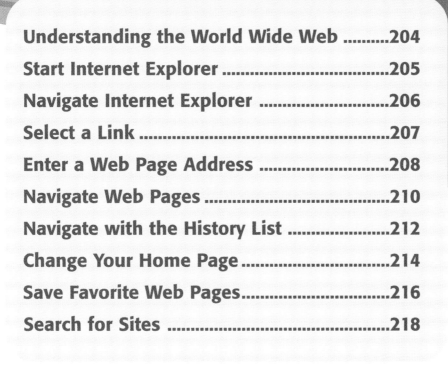

The World Wide Web — the Web, for short — is a massive storehouse of information that resides on computers, called *Web servers*, located all over the world.

Web Page

World Wide Web information is presented on Web pages, which you download to your computer using a Web browser program, such as Windows XP's Internet Explorer. Each Web page can combine text with images, sounds, music, and even videos to present you with information on a particular subject. The Web consists of billions of pages covering almost every imaginable topic.

Web Site

A Web site is a collection of Web pages associated with a particular person, business, government, school, or organization. Web sites are stored on a Web server, a special computer that makes Web pages available for people to browse.

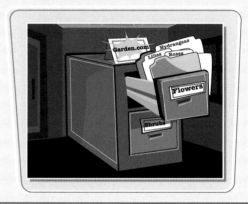

Web Address

Every Web page has its own Web address that uniquely identifies the page. This address is sometimes called a URL (pronounced *yoo-ar-ell* or *erl*), which is short for Uniform Resource Locator. If you know the address of a page, you can plug that address into your Web browser to view the page.

Links

A link is a kind of "cross-reference" to another Web page. Each link is a bit of text (usually shown underlined and in a different color) or an image that, when you click it, loads the other page into your Web browser automatically. The other page is often from the same site, but it is common to come across links that take you to pages anywhere on the Web.

Start Internet Explorer

You can use Internet Explorer, Windows XP's built-in Web browser program, to surf the Web. To do this, you must first start Internet Explorer.

Start Internet Explorer

① Connect to the Internet.

② Click **start**.

③ Click **Internet**.

Note: *If your computer is set up so that the Internet item on the Start menu launches some other browser, click* **All Programs**, *and then click* **Internet Explorer**.

The Internet Explorer window appears.

● When you are finished with the Web, click Close (⊠) to shut down Internet Explorer.

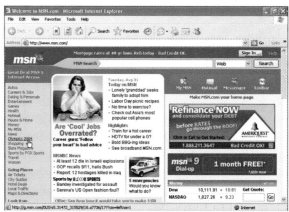

Navigate Internet Explorer

You can easily surf the Web if you know your way around the Internet Explorer Web browser.

Web Page Title
This part of the Internet Explorer title bar displays the title of the displayed Web page.

Address Bar
This text box displays the address of the displayed Web page. You can also use the Address bar to type the address of a Web page that you want to visit.

Links
Links appear either as text or as images. On most pages (although not the page shown here), text links appear underlined and in a different color (usually blue) than the regular page text.

Current Link
This is the link that you are currently pointing at with your mouse. The mouse pointer changes from ⟶ to 👆. On some pages (such as the one shown here), the link text also becomes underlined and changes color.

Status Bar
This area displays the current status of Internet Explorer. For example, it displays *Opening page* when you are downloading a Web page, and *Done* when the page is fully loaded. When you point at a link, the Status bar displays the address of the page associated with the link.

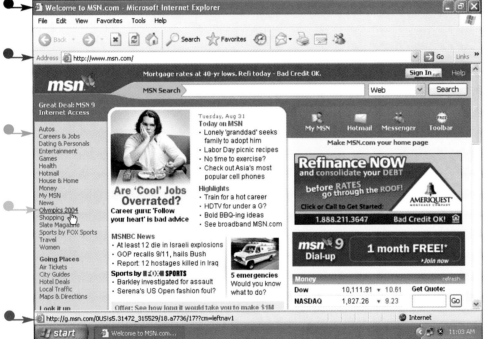

Select a Link

Almost all Web pages include links to other pages that contain information related to something in the current page, and you can use these links to navigate to other Web pages. When you select a link, your Web browser loads the other page.

Knowing which words, phrases, or images are links is not always obvious. The only way to tell for sure in many cases is to position the ⬚ over the text or image; if the ⬚ changes to a ⬚, you know you are dealing with a link.

Select a Link

① Position the ⬚ over the link (⬚ changes to ⬚).

② Click the text or image.

● The Status bar shows the current download status.

Note: The address shown in the Status bar when you point at a link may be different than the one shown when the page is downloading. This happens when the Web site "redirects" the link, which happens frequently.

The linked Web page appears.

● The Web page title and address change after the linked page is loaded.

Enter a Web Page Address

If you know the address of a specific Web page, you can type that address into the Web browser and the program will display the page.

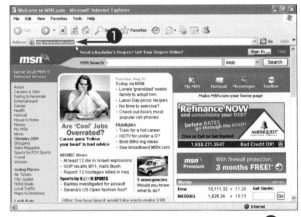

Enter a Web Page Address

① Click inside the Address bar.

② Type the address of the Web page.

③ Click ➔.

The Web page appears.

● The Web page title changes after the page is loaded.

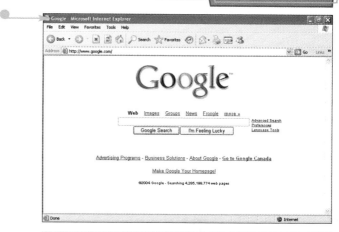

REDISPLAY A WEB PAGE

① Click ▾ in the Address bar.

A list of the addresses you have typed appears.

② Click the address you want to display.

The Web page appears.

*Note: If you type the first few letters of the address (such as **goog**), the Address bar displays a list of addresses that match what you have typed. If you see the address you want, click it to load the page.*

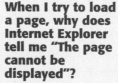
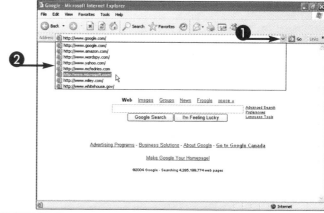

Are there any shortcuts I can use to enter Web page addresses?

Here are some useful keyboard techniques:

● After you finish typing the address, press Enter instead of clicking ▸.

● Most Web addresses begin with *http://*. You can leave off these characters when you type your address; Internet Explorer adds them automatically.

● If the address uses the form http://www.something. com, type just the "something" part and press Ctrl + Enter. Internet Explorer automatically adds *http://www.* at the beginning and *.com* at the end.

When I try to load a page, why does Internet Explorer tell me "The page cannot be displayed"?

This message means that Internet Explorer is unable to contact a Web server at the address you typed. This is often a temporary glitch, so click ▸ to try loading the page again. If the trouble persists, double-check your address to ensure that you typed it correctly. If you did, the site may be unavailable for some reason. Try again in a few hours.

Navigate Web Pages

After you have visited several pages, you can return to a page you visited earlier. Rather than retyping the address or looking for the link, Internet Explorer gives you some easier methods.

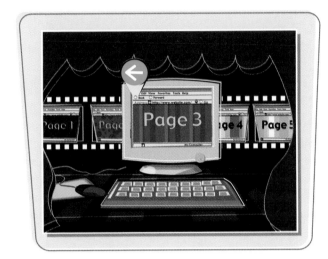

When you navigate Web pages, you can go back to a page you have visited in the current browser session. After you have done that, you can also reverse course and go forward through the pages again.

Navigate Web Pages

GO BACK ONE PAGE

1 Click ⬅.

The previous page you visited appears.

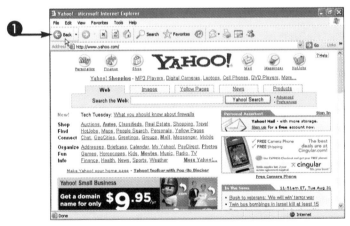

GO BACK SEVERAL PAGES

1 Click ⬇ in the Back list.

A list of the sites you have visited appears.

2 Click the page you want to display.

The page appears.

GO FORWARD ONE PAGE

① Click .

The next page you visited appears.

Note: If you are at the last page viewed up to that point, the icon is not active.

GO FORWARD SEVERAL PAGES

① Click ⬚ in the Forward list.

A list of the sites you have visited appears.

② Click the page you want to display.

The page appears.

TIP

How do I go back or forward to a page, but also keep the current page on-screen?

You can do this by opening a second Internet Explorer window. Keep the current page in the original window and then use the second window to go back or forward. Here are the steps to follow:

① Click **File**.

② Click **New**.

③ Click **Window**.

A copy of the Internet Explorer window appears.

④ Use the Back or Forward buttons in the new window to navigate to the page you want.

Navigate with the History List

The Back and Forward buttons enable you only to navigate pages in the current browser session. To redisplay sites that you have visited in the past few days or weeks, you need to use the History list.

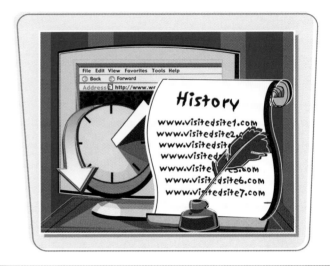

Navigate with the History List

1 Click .

● The History list appears.

2 Click the day or week that you visited the site.

A list of sites that you visited during that day or week appears.

③ Click the site that contains the page you want to display.

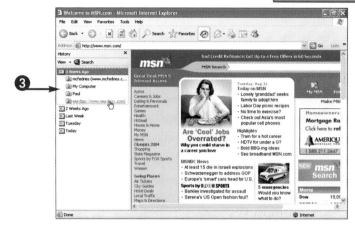

A list of pages you visited in the site appears.

④ Click the page you want to display.

● The page appears.

⑤ When you are done, click ✕ to close the History list.

TIPS

Can I control the number of days that Internet Explorer keeps track of the pages I visit?

Yes, by following these steps:

① Click **Tools**.

② Click **Internet Options**.

③ Use the **Days to keep pages in history** spin box to set the number of days (the maximum is 99).

④ Click **OK**.

Can I clear my History list?

Yes, by following these steps:

① Click **Tools**.

② Click **Internet Options**.

③ Click **Clear History**.

Internet Explorer asks if you are sure you want to delete your history.

④ Click **Yes**.

⑤ Click **OK**.

Change Your Home Page

Your home page is the Web page that appears when you first start Internet Explorer. The default home page is the MSN.com site, but you can change that to any other page you want.

Your version of Internet Explorer may not use MSN.com as the default home page. For example, some computer manufacturers set up their own sites as the default home page.

Change Your Home Page

① Display the Web page that you want to use as your home page.

② Click **Tools**.

③ Click **Internet Options**.

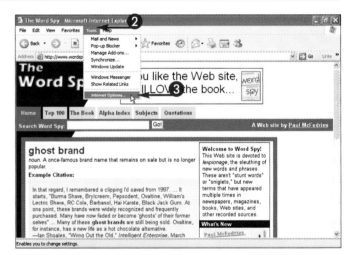

The Internet Options dialog box appears.

④ Click **Use Current**.

● The Web address of the page appears in the Address text box.

5 Click **OK**.

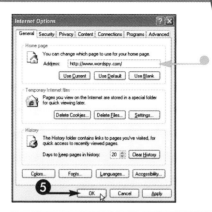

DISPLAY YOUR HOME PAGE

1 Click 🏠.

Your home page appears.

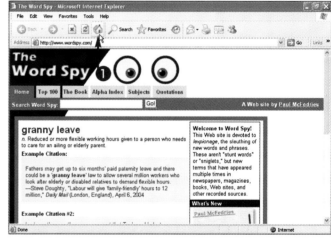

Can I return to using MSN.com as my home page?

Yes, by following these steps:

1 Click **Tools**.

2 Click **Internet Options**.

3 Click **Use Default**.

4 Click **OK**.

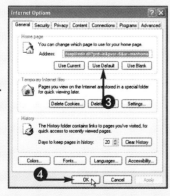

Can I get Internet Explorer to load without displaying a home page?

Yes, by following these steps:

1 Click **Tools**.

2 Click **Internet Options**.

3 Click **Use Blank**.

4 Click **OK**.

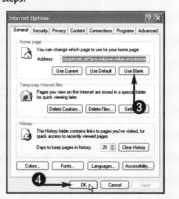

Save Favorite
Web Pages

If you have Web pages that you visit frequently, you can save yourself time by saving those pages as favorites within Internet Explorer. This enables you to display the pages with just a couple of mouse clicks.

The Favorites feature is a list of Web pages that you have saved. Rather than typing an address or searching for one of these pages, you can display the Web page by selecting its address from the Favorites list.

Save Favorite Web Pages

① Display the Web page you want to save as a favorite.

② Click **Favorites**.

③ Click **Add To Favorites**.

The Add Favorite dialog box appears.

④ Edit the page name, as necessary.

⑤ Click **OK**.

DISPLAY A FAVORITE WEB PAGE

1 Click **Favorites**.

The Favorites list appears.

2 Click the Web page you want to display.

The Web page appears.

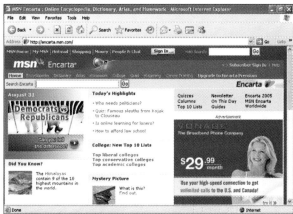

TIPS

I use my Favorites list a lot. Is there an easier way to display these pages?

Yes. To keep the Favorites list visible, follow these steps:

1 Click ⭐.

The Favorites list appears on the left side of the Internet Explorer window.

2 Click the page you want to display.

How do I delete a favorite?

1 Click **Favorites**.

2 Right-click the favorite you want to delete.

3 Click **Delete**.

Internet Explorer asks if you are sure you want to delete the favorite.

4 Click **Yes**.

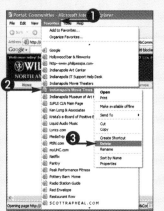

If you need information on a specific topic, Internet Explorer has a built-in feature that enables you to quickly search the Web for sites that have the information you require.

The Web has a number of sites called *search engines* that enable you to find what you are looking for. By default, Internet Explorer uses the MSN Search site, but you can use other sites.

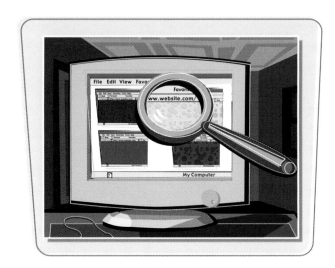

1 Click 🔍.

● The Search Companion appears.

2 Click the text box, and then type a word, phrase, or question that represents the information you want to find.

3 Click **Search**.

● A list of pages that match your search text appears.

④ Click a Web page.

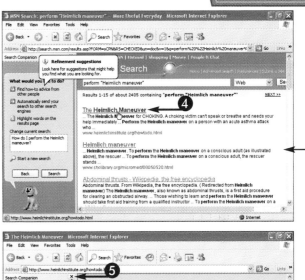

● The page appears.

⑤ When you are done, click ☒ to close the Search Companion.

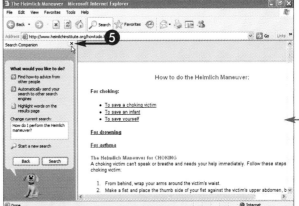

TIP

Can I use other search engines?

Yes. Type the search engine address into Internet Explorer and then use the page that appears to perform your search. Here are the addresses of some popular search engines:

Google	www.google.com
AltaVista	www.altavista.com
Ask Jeeves	www.ask.com
Excite	www.excite.com
HotBot	www.hotbot.com
Yahoo!	www.yahoo.com

Sending and
Receiving E-mail

You can use Windows XP's
Outlook Express program to
send e-mail to and read
e-mail from friends, family,
colleagues, and even total
strangers almost anywhere
in the world. This chapter
shows you how to perform
these and many more
e-mail tasks.

Start Outlook Express

With Outlook Express, the e-mail program that comes with Windows XP, you can send or receive e-mail messages. You must first launch Outlook Express.

Start Outlook Express

① Connect to the Internet.

② Click **start**.

③ Click **E-mail**.

Note: If your computer is set up so that the E-mail item on the Start menu launches some other program, click **All Programs**, and then click **Outlook Express**.

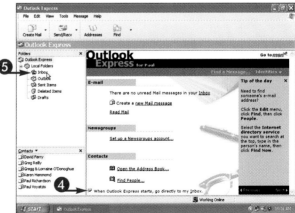

The Outlook Express window appears.

④ Click **When Outlook Express starts, go directly to my Inbox** (☐ changes to ☑).

⑤ Click **Inbox**.

The Inbox folder appears.

Note: Your Inbox displays automatically the next time you start Outlook Express, so you can skip step **5**.

When you finish your e-mail chores, click Close (☒) to shut down Outlook Express.

Outlook Express makes e-mailing easy, but you can make it even easier by taking a few moments now to learn the layout of the Outlook Express window.

Folder List

This area lists the five storage folders that Outlook Express provides. You use these folders to store various types of messages; you can also create your own folders. The five folders are:

◉ Inbox stores your incoming messages. To learn how to get your messages, see the section "Receive and Read E-mail Messages" in this chapter.

◉ Outbox stores outgoing messages that you have not yet sent. To learn how to send messages, see the section "Send an E-mail Message" in this chapter.

◉ Sent Items stores outgoing messages that you have sent.

● Deleted Items stores messages that you have deleted from some other folder.

● Drafts stores messages that you saved but have not yet finished composing.

Current Folder

This bar tells you the name of the folder that is currently selected in the folder list.

Messages

This area shows a list of the messages that are contained in the current folder.

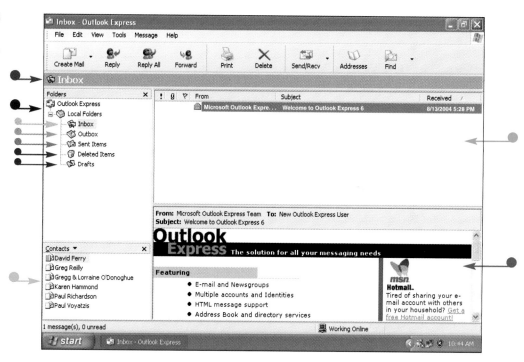

Contacts

This area lists the people you have added to your Address Book. The Contacts list is usually empty when you first start using Outlook Express. To populate the Contacts list, see the section "Add a Contact to Your Address Book" in this chapter.

Preview Pane

This area shows a preview of the currently selected message.

Send an E-mail Message

If you know the e-mail address of a person or organization, you can send an e-mail message to that address. In most cases, the message is delivered within a few minutes.

If you do not know any e-mail addresses, or if at first you prefer to just practice sending messages, you can send messages to your own e-mail address.

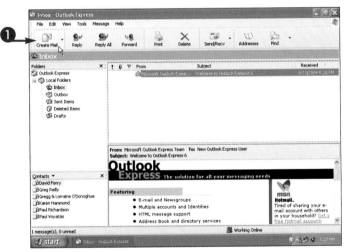

Send an E-mail Message

① Click **Create Mail**.

A message window appears.

② Type the e-mail address of the person to whom you are sending the message.

③ To send a copy of the message to another person, type that person's e-mail address.

Note: You can add multiple e-mail addresses in both the To line and the Cc line. Separate each address with a semicolon (;).

④ Type a title or short description for the message.

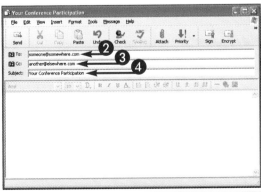

⑤ Type the message.

⑥ Use the buttons in the Formatting bar and the Format menu to format the message text.

Note: *Many people use e-mail programs that cannot process text formatting. Unless you are sure your recipient's program supports formatting, it is best to send plain text messages. To do this, click* **Format** *and then click* **Plain Text** *(■ appears beside the command).*

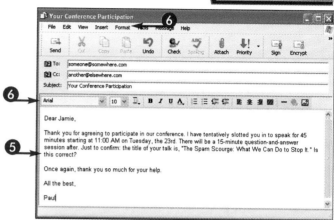

⑦ Click **Send**.

Outlook Express sends your message.

Note: *Outlook Express stores a copy of your message in the Sent Items folder.*

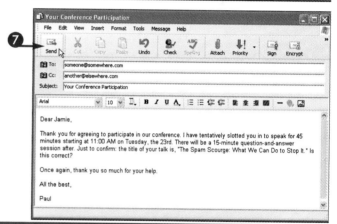

I have a large number of messages to compose. Do I have to be online to do this?

No, composing all the messages while you are offline is possible. Follow these steps:

① While disconnected from the Internet, start Outlook Express, and click **Cancel** if the program asks you to connect to the Internet.

② To ensure you are working offline, click **File**. Click the **Work Offline** command if you do not see ✔ beside it.

③ Compose and send the message. Each time you click **Send**, your messages are stored temporarily in the **Outbox** folder.

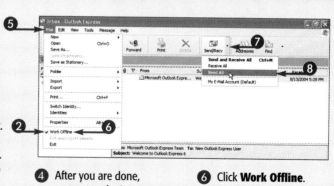

④ After you are done, connect to the Internet.

⑤ Click **File**.

⑥ Click **Work Offline**.

⑦ Click · in the **Send/Recv** toolbar button.

⑧ Click **Send All**.

Add a Contact to the Address Book

You can use your address book to store the names and addresses of people with whom you frequently correspond.

When you choose a name from the address book while composing a message, Outlook Express automatically adds the contact's e-mail address. This is both faster and more accurate than typing the address by hand.

Add a Contact to the Address Book

① Click **Addresses**.

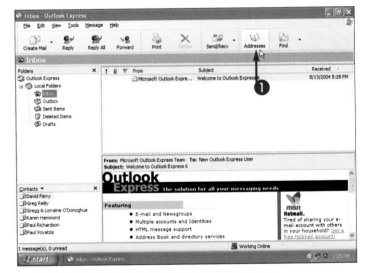

The Address Book window appears.

② Click **New**.

③ Click **New Contact**.

The Properties dialog box appears.

Note: *A quicker way to display the Properties dialog box is to click* **Contacts** *in the Outlook Express window, and then click* **New Contact**.

④ Type the person's first name.

⑤ Type the person's last name.

⑥ Type the person's e-mail address.

⑦ Click **OK**.

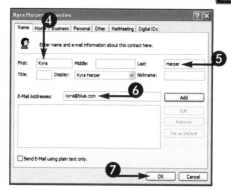

● The address is added to the Address Book and to the Contacts list.

Note: *You can use the other tabs in the Properties dialog box to store more information about the contact, including home and business addresses and phone numbers, spouse and children names, birthday, and more.*

⑧ Click ☒ to close the Address Book window.

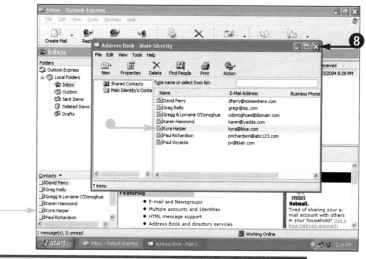

How do I change a person's e-mail address?

① In the Address Book window, double-click the person's name to open the Properties dialog box.

② Click the **Name** tab.

③ Click **Edit**.

④ Type the new address.

⑤ Click **OK**.

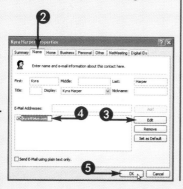

How do I delete someone from the address book?

① In the Address Book window, click the person's name that you want to delete.

② Click **Delete**.

The address book asks if you are sure.

③ Click **Yes**.

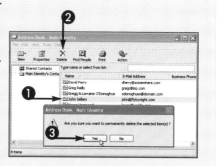

Select an Address Book Address

After you have some e-mail addresses and names in your address book, you can select the address you want from your list of contacts instead of typing the address when composing a message.

Select an Address Book Address

① Click **Create Mail** to start a new message.

② Click **To**.

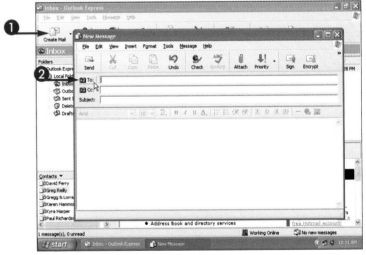

The Select Recipients dialog box appears.

③ Click the person to whom you want to send the message.

④ Click **To**.

● The person's name appears in the Message recipients box.

⑤ Repeat steps **3** and **4** to add other recipients to the To line.

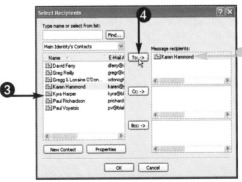

6 To send a copy of the message to a recipient, click the person's name.

7 Click **Cc**.

● The person's name appears in the Message recipients box.

8 Repeat steps **6** and **7** to add other recipients to the Cc line.

Note: The *Bcc* button sends a blind courtesy copy, which means addresses added here are not displayed to the other recipients.

9 Click **OK**.

● Outlook Express adds the recipients to the To and Cc lines of the new message.

Note: You only see the Bcc line if you added a Bcc recipient. Alternatively, click View, All Headers to display the Bcc line.

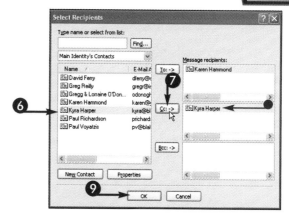

How do I use the Contacts list?

The Contacts list is handy for quickly sending a message to a single person. When you double-click a name in the Contacts list, Outlook Express creates a new message and automatically places the recipient's name in the To line. You can also make changes to the contact's information: Right-click the contact name, and then click Properties. To delete a contact, right-click the name, and then click Delete.

● Double-click the recipient's name.

● A new message appears with the recipient's name filled in automatically.

Add a File Attachment

If you have a memo, image, or other document that you want to send to another person, you can attach the document to an e-mail message. The other person can then open the document after he or she receives your message.

Add a File Attachment

① Click **Create Mail** to start a new message.

② Click **Attach**.

The Insert Attachment dialog box appears.

③ Click the file you want to attach.

④ Click **Attach**.

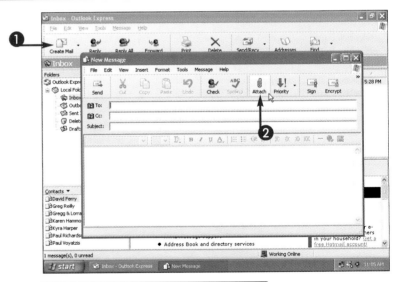

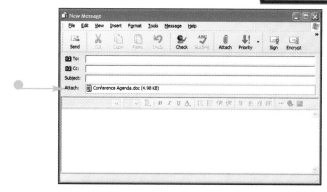

● Outlook Express attaches the file to the message.

5 Repeat steps **2** to **4** to attach additional files to the message.

CLICK AND DRAG AN ATTACHMENT

1 Click **Create Mail** to start a new message.

2 Open My Documents, or whatever folder contains the file you want to attach.

3 Click and drag the file from the folder and drop it inside the message text area.

4 Outlook Express attaches the file to the message.

Is there a limit to the number of files I can attach to a message?

There is no practical limit to the number of files you can attach to the message. However, you should be careful with the total *size* of the files you send. If you or the recipient has a slow Internet connection, sending or receiving the message can take an extremely long time. Also, many ISPs place a limit on the size of a message's attachments, which is usually around 2 MB. In general, use e-mail to send only a few small files at a time.

Add a Signature

In an e-mail message, a *signature* is a small amount of text that appears at the bottom of the message. Rather than typing this information manually, you can create the signature once and then have Outlook Express automatically add the signature to any message you send.

Signatures usually contain personal contact information, such as your phone numbers, business address, and e-mail and Web site addresses. Some people supplement their signatures with wise or witty quotations.

Add a Signature

① Click **Tools**.

② Click **Options**.

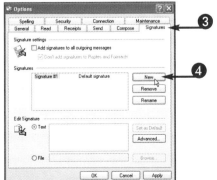

The Options dialog box appears.

③ Click the **Signatures** tab.

④ Click **New**.

Outlook Express adds a new signature.

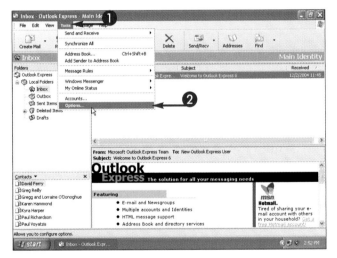

⑤ Type the signature text.

⑥ Click **OK**.

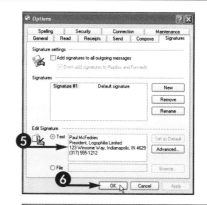

INSERT THE SIGNATURE MANUALLY

① Click **Create Mail** to start a new message.

② In the message text area, move the insertion point to the location where you want the signature to appear.

③ Click **Insert**.

④ Click **Signature**.

Note: If you have more than one signature, click the one you want to use from the menu that appears.

● The signature appears in the message.

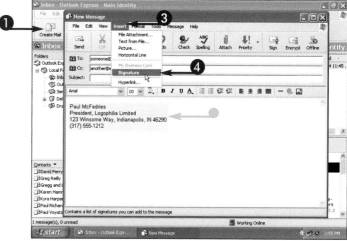

TIPS

Can I have more than one signature?

Yes, you can add as many signatures as you want. For example, you may want to have one signature with your business contact information and another with your personal contact information. To avoid confusing these signatures, give each one a descriptive name. For each signature, follow these steps:

① Click the signature.

② Click **Rename**.

③ Type the new name.

④ Press Enter.

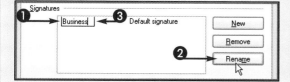

Can I get Outlook Express to add my signature automatically?

Yes. Two options in the Signatures tab control this:

● Click **Add signatures to all outgoing messages** (☐ changes to ☑) to have Outlook Express add your signature to the bottom of every new message.

● Click **Don't add signatures to Replies and Forwards** (☑ changes to ☐) if you want Outlook Express to add your signature when you reply to and forward messages.

Receive and Read E-mail Messages

A message sent to you by another person is stored on your ISP's e-mail server computer. You must connect to the ISP's computer to retrieve and read the message. As you see in this section, Outlook Express does most of the work for you automatically.

Outlook Express automatically checks for new messages when you start the program, and then checks for more messages every 30 minutes while you are online.

Receive and Read E-mail Messages

RECEIVE E-MAIL MESSAGES

① Click ⊡ in the **Send/Recv** toolbar button.

② Click **Receive All**.

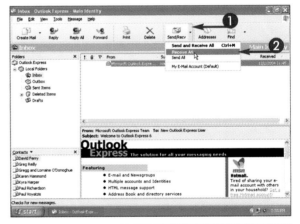

● If you have new messages, they appear in your Inbox folder in bold type.

● Whenever a new message arrives, the 🔍 icon appears in the taskbar's notification area.

● This symbol means that the message came with a file attached.

● This symbol means the message was sent as high priority.

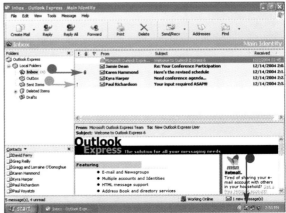

READ A MESSAGE

1 Click the message.

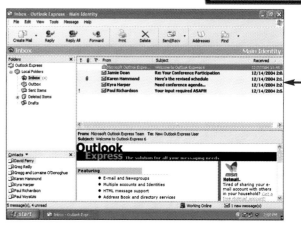

2 Read the message text in the preview pane.

Note: I you want to open the message in its own window, double-click the message.

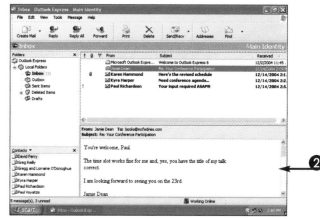

TIP

Can I change how often Outlook Express automatically checks for messages?

1 Click **Tools**.

2 Click **Options**.

The Options dialog box appears.

3 Click the **General** tab.

4 If you do not want Outlook Express to check for messages when the program starts, click **Send and receive messages at startup** (☑ changes to ☐).

5 Type a new time interval, in minutes, that you want Outlook Express to use when checking for new messages automatically.

6 Click **OK**.

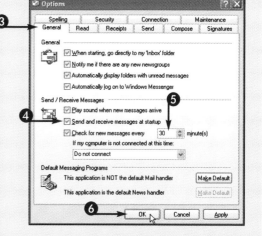

Reply to a Message

When a message you receive requires some kind of response — whether it is answering a question, supplying information, or providing comments or criticisms — you can reply to any message you receive.

Reply to a Message

① Click the message to which you want to reply.

② Click the reply type you want to use:

Click **Reply** to respond only to the first address displayed on the To line.

Click **Reply All** to respond to all the addresses in the To and Cc lines.

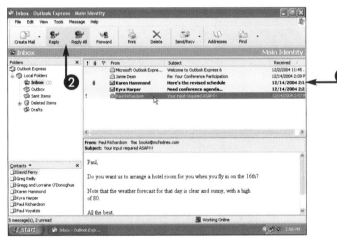

A message window appears.

● Outlook Express automatically inserts the recipient addresses.

● Outlook Express also inserts the subject line, preceded by Re:.

● Outlook Express includes the original message's addresses (To and From), date, subject, and text at the bottom of the reply.

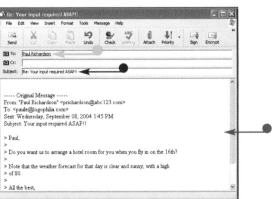

3 Edit the original message to include only the text that is relevant to your reply.

Note: *If the original message was fairly short, you usually do not need to edit the text. However, if the original message was long, and your response deals only with part of that message, you will save the recipient time by deleting everything except the relevant portion of the text.*

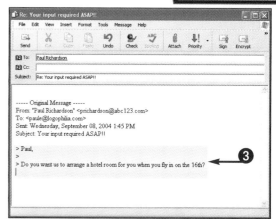

4 Click the area above the original message text and type your reply.

5 Click **Send**.

Outlook Express sends your reply.

Note: *Outlook Express stores a copy of your reply in the Sent Items folder.*

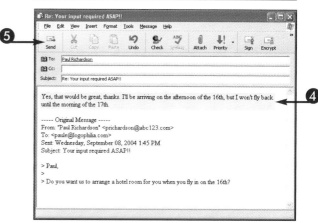

Each time I reply to a message, Outlook Express adds the recipient to my Contacts list. How do I prevent this?

1 Click **Tools**.

2 Click **Options**.

The Options dialog box appears.

3 Click the **Send** tab.

4 Click **Automatically put people I reply to in my Address Book** (☑ changes to ☐).

5 Click **OK**.

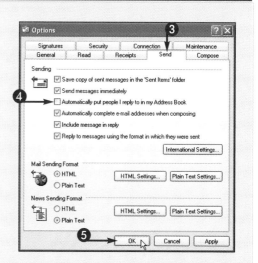

Forward a Message

If a message has information that is relevant to or concerns another person, you can forward a copy of that message to the other recipient. You can also include your own comments in the forward.

Forward a Message

1 Click the message that you want to forward.

2 Click **Forward**.

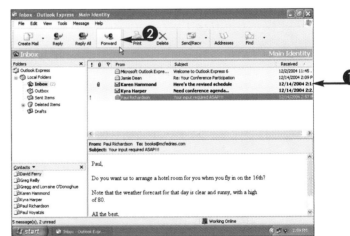

A message window appears.

● Outlook Express inserts the subject line, preceded by Fw:.

● The original message's addresses (To and From), date, subject, and text are included at the bottom of the forward.

3 Type the e-mail address of the person to whom you are forwarding the message.

4 To send a copy of the forward to another person, type that person's e-mail address.

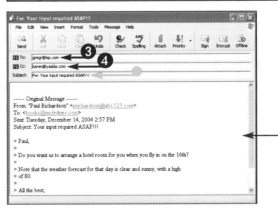

⑤ Edit the original message to include only the text that is relevant to your forward.

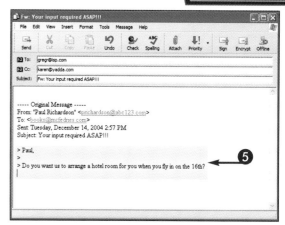

⑥ Click the area above the original message text and type your comments.

⑦ Click **Send**.

Outlook Express sends your forward.

Note: *Outlook Express stores a copy of your forward in the Sent Items folder.*

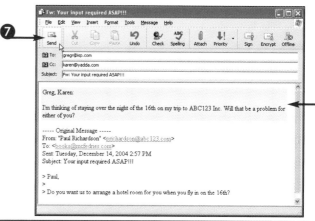

How do I forward someone a copy of the actual message instead of just a copy of the message text?

Click the message, click **Message**, and then click **Forward As Attachment**. Outlook Express creates a new message and includes the original message as an attachment.

My replies and forwards don't always use the same format. How can I make Outlook Express use a single format?

① Click **Tools**.

② Click **Options**.

The Options dialog box appears.

③ Click the **Send** tab.

④ Click here (☑ changes to ☐).

⑤ Click the format you want.

⑥ Click **OK**.

Open and Save an Attachment

If you receive a message that has a file attached, you can open the attachment to view the contents of the file. You can also save the attachment as a file on your computer.

Be careful when dealing with attached files. Computer viruses are often transmitted by e-mail attachments. See the section "Protect against Viruses" in this chapter.

Open and Save an Attachment

OPEN AN ATTACHMENT

① Click the message that has the attachment, as indicated by the 🔟 icon.

② In the preview pane, click 📎.

A list of the message attachments appears.

③ Click the attachment you want to open.

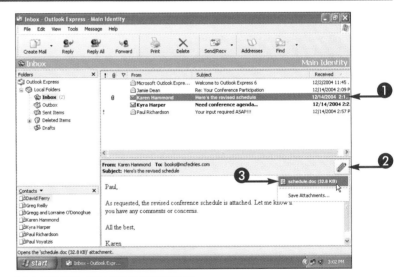

Outlook Express asks you to confirm that you want to open the file.

④ Click **Open**.

The file opens in the appropriate program.

Note: Instead of opening the file, Windows XP may display a dialog box telling that the file "does not have a program associated with it." This means you need to install the appropriate program for the type of file. If you are not sure, ask the person who sent you the file what program you need.

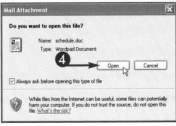

SAVE AN ATTACHMENT

① Click the message that has the attachment, as indicated by the 🔗 icon.

② In the preview pane, click 📎.

A list of the message attachments appears.

③ Click **Save Attachments**.

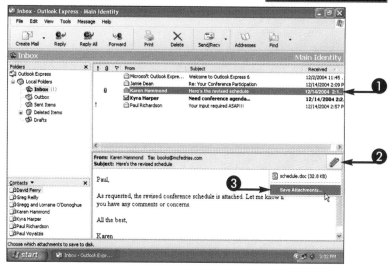

The Save Attachments dialog box appears.

④ Click the file you want to save.

⑤ Type the name of the folder into which you want the file saved.

⑥ Click **Save**.

TIP

When I click 📎, why can't I click either the file name or the Save Attachments command?

Outlook Express has determined that the attached file may be unsafe, meaning that the file may harbor a virus or other malicious code. To confirm this, double-click the message to open it. Below the toolbar, you should see a message saying, "OE removed access to the following unsafe attachments in your mail." To learn how to turn off this feature, see "Protect against Viruses" in this chapter.

● This message appears when Outlook Express blocks an unsafe attachment.

Create a Folder for Saving Messages

After you have used Outlook Express for a while, you may find that you have many messages in your Inbox folder. To keep the Inbox uncluttered, you can create new folders and then move messages from the Inbox to the new folders.

You should use each folder you create to save related messages. For example, you could create separate folders for people you correspond with regularly, projects you are working on, different work departments, and so on.

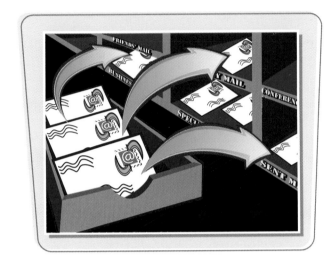

Create a Folder for Saving Messages

CREATE A FOLDER

1 Click either Local Folders or the folder in which you want to create the new folder.

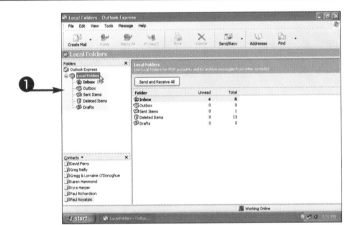

2 Click **File**.

3 Click **Folder**.

4 Click **New**.

The Create Folder dialog box appears.

⑤ Type the name of the new folder.

⑥ Click **OK**.

The new folder appears in the Folders list.

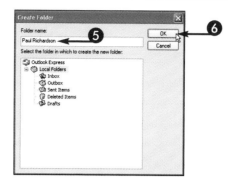

MOVE A MESSAGE TO ANOTHER FOLDER

① Click the folder that contains the message you want to move.

② Position the ⬚ over the message you want to move.

③ Click and drag the message and drop it on the folder to which you want to move the message.

Outlook Express moves the message.

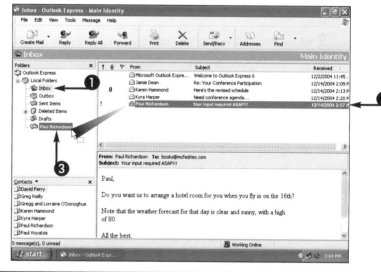

 TIPS

How do I rename a folder?

Click the folder and then click **File**, **Folder**, and **Rename**. Use the Rename Folder dialog box to type the new name and then click **OK**. Note that Outlook Express only allows you to rename those folders that you have created yourself.

How do I delete a folder?

Click the folder and then click **File**, **Folder**, and **Delete**. When Outlook Express asks you to confirm the deletion, click **Yes**. Note that Outlook Express only allows you to delete those folders that you have created yourself. Remember, too, that when you delete a folder, you also delete any messages stored in that folder.

Create Rules to Filter Incoming Messages

You can make your e-mail chores faster and more efficient if you create *rules* that handle incoming messages automatically.

A rule combines a condition and an action. The condition is one or more message criteria, such as the address of the sender or words in the subject line. The action is what happens to a message that satisfies the condition, such as moving the message to another folder or sending a reply.

Filter Incoming Messages

1 Click **Tools**.

2 Click **Message Rules**.

3 Click **Mail**.

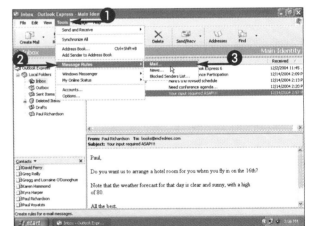

4 If the Message Rules dialog box appears, click **New**.

The New Mail Rule dialog box appears.

5 Under Select the Conditions for your rule, click the condition you want to use (☐ changes to ☑).

6 If the condition requires editing, click the underlined text in the Rule Description box.

A dialog box appears, the layout of which depends on the condition.

7 Enter the text, address, or other required information.

8 Click **Add**.

9 Repeat steps **6** and **7** to add other data to the rule.

10 Click **OK**.

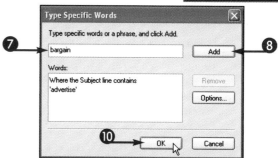

11 Under Select the Actions for your rule, click the action you want to use (□ changes to ☑).

12 If the action requires editing, follow steps **5** to **8**.

13 Type a name for the rule.

14 Click **OK**.

Outlook Express adds the rule to the Message Rules dialog box.

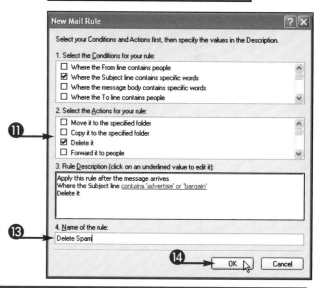

TIPS

Can I use a rule to automatically delete spam?

Yes. Spam, or unsolicited commercial e-mail, often comes with predictable words and phrases in the subject line. In your rule, activate the **Where the Subject line contains specific words** condition and the **Delete it** action. For the condition, add the spam-related words and phrases, such as the following: advertise, bargain, casino, diploma, get out of debt, millionaire, Viagra, work from home.

How do I make changes to a rule?

1 Follow steps **1** to **3** from "Filter Incoming Messages."

2 Click the rule you want to change.

3 Click **Modify**.

The Edit Mail Rule dialog box appears.

4 Make your changes to the rule.

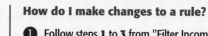

Protect against Viruses

Many computer viruses — small programs that can damage your computer — are transmitted via e-mail. You can protect your computer from this malicious code by setting a few Outlook Express options.

Protect against Viruses

1 Click **Tools**.

2 Click **Options**.

The Options dialog box appears.

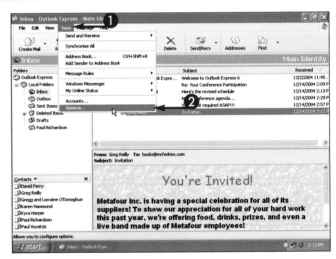

3 Click the **Read** tab.

4 Click **Read all messages in plain text** (☐ changes to ☑).

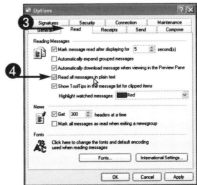

5 Click the **Security** tab.

6 Click **Restricted sites zone** (○ changes to ⦿).

7 Click **Warn me when other applications try to send mail as me** (☐ changes to ☑).

8 Click **Do not allow attachments to be saved or opened that could potentially be a virus** (☐ changes to ☑).

9 Click **Block images and other external content in HTML e-mail** (☐ changes to ☑).

10 Click **OK**.

● When you click ✐ with Outlook Express set up to block potentially unsafe attachments, the file names and Save Attachments command become unavailable.

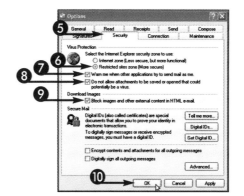

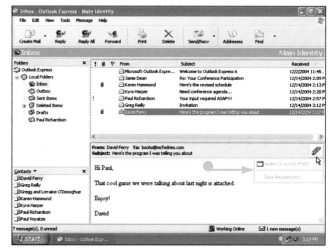

Is there an easy way to view images and HTML formatting if I have those options turned off?

1 Click the message.

2 Click **View**.

3 Click **Blocked Images** to see the blocked images.

4 Click **Message in HTML** to see the blocked HTML.

Are there other ways that I can protect my computer against e-mail viruses?

Yes.

● When a message has an attachment and you do not know the sender of the message or recognize the file type of the attachment, do not open the attachment.

● When you get an attachment unexpectedly, write the sender back to confirm that he or she actually sent it.

● Install a good antivirus program on your system; a program that checks incoming messages for viruses is a must.

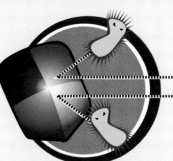

Customizing
Windows XP

Windows XP comes with a
number of features that
enable you to personalize
your computer. Not only
can you change the
appearance of Windows XP
to suit your taste, but you
can also change the way
Windows XP works to
make it easier and more
efficient.

Open the Display Properties

To make changes to Windows XP's Display Properties dialog box, you need to know how to open this dialog box.

① Click **start**.

② Click **Control Panel**.

The Control Panel window appears.

③ Click **Appearance and Themes**.

The Appearance and Themes window appears.

④ Click **Display**.

● The Display Properties dialog box appears.

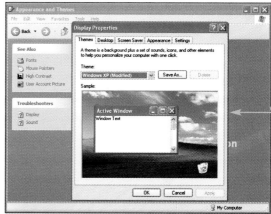

TIP

**Is there a quicker way to open
the Display Properties dialog box?**

Yes. Follow these steps:

❶ Right-click an empty section of the desktop.

❷ Click **Properties**.

The Display Properties dialog box appears.

Change the Desktop Background

For a different look, you can change the desktop background to display either a different image or a specific color.

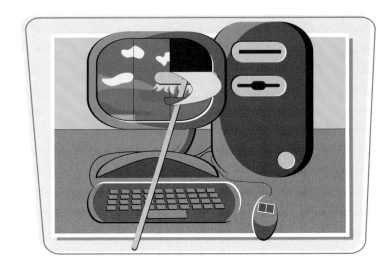

CHANGE THE BACKGROUND IMAGE

1 Open the Display Properties dialog box.

Note: *See the section "Open the Display Properties" earlier in this chapter.*

2 Click the **Desktop** tab.

3 Click the image you want to use as the desktop background.

● A preview of the desktop background appears.

4 Click ☑ in the Position list and then click a display method for the image.

5 Click **OK** (or click **Apply** to leave the dialog box onscreen).

The picture you selected appears on the desktop.

Note: *If you have your own image that you would prefer to use as the desktop background, click **Browse** and then use the Browse dialog box to select the file.*

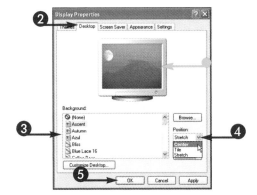

CHANGE THE BACKGROUND COLOR

1 Open the Display Properties dialog box.

Note: See the section "Open the Display Properties" earlier in this chapter.

2 Click the **Desktop** tab.

3 In the Background list, click **None**.

4 Click **Color**.

A palette of colors appears.

5 Click the color you want to use for the desktop background.

6 Click **OK** (or click **Apply** to leave the dialog box onscreen).

The color appears on the desktop.

*Note: To create a custom color, click **Other** in the color palette and then use the Color dialog box to choose the color you want.*

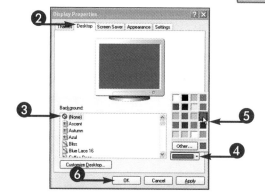

What is the difference between the three Position options?

Center

The center option, which is the Windows XP default setting, displays the image in the center of the desktop.

Tile

If you select the Tile option, your image repeats multiple times to fill the entire desktop.

Stretch

The stretch option expands the image to fill the entire desktop. This option can distort the image.

Set the Screen Saver

You can set up Windows XP to display a *screen saver*, a moving pattern or series of pictures. The screen saver appears after your computer has been idle for a while.

If you leave your monitor on for long stretches while your computer is idle, the unmoving image can end up "burned" into the monitor's screen. A screen saver prevents this by displaying a moving image.

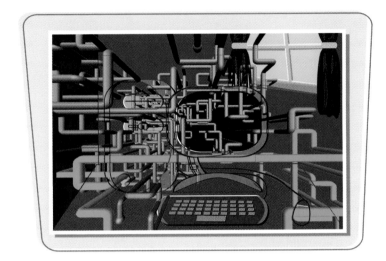

Set the Screen Saver

1 Open the Display Properties dialog box.

Note: See the section "Open the Display Properties" earlier in this chapter.

2 Click the **Screen Saver** tab.

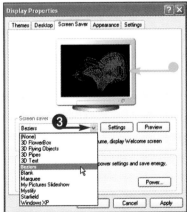

3 Click ⬇ in the **Screen Saver** list and then click the screen saver you want to use.

● A preview of the screen saver appears.

*Note: Not all screen savers can display the small preview. To see an actual preview, click **Preview**. When you are done, move the mouse or press a key to stop the preview.*

④ Click 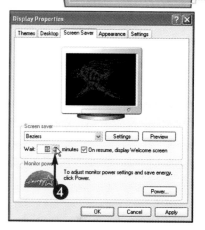 in the **Wait** spin box to specify the number of minutes of computer idle time after which the screen saver appears.

⑤ Click **OK** (or click **Apply** to leave the dialog box onscreen).

The screen saver appears after your computer is idle for the number of minutes you specified in step **4**.

Note: To interrupt the screen saver, move your mouse or press a key on your keyboard.

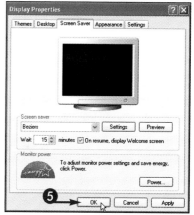

TIP

Can I use a screen saver to hide my work while I am away from my desk?

Yes. By itself, the screen saver's pattern automatically obscures the screen. However, another person can interrupt the screen saver to see your work. To prevent this, first assign a password to your Windows XP user account, as described in the section "Protect an Account with a Password" in Chapter 7. In the **Screen Saver** tab, make sure you leave the check box labeled "On Resume, Display Welcome Screen" activated. This means that anyone who interrupts the screen saver can only see your work if they know your password.

Change the Windows XP Colors and Fonts

You can personalize your copy of Windows XP by changing the overall style of the windows and buttons, by choosing a different color scheme, and by applying a different font size.

If you find that you have trouble reading the regular Windows XP text, choose one of the larger font sizes.

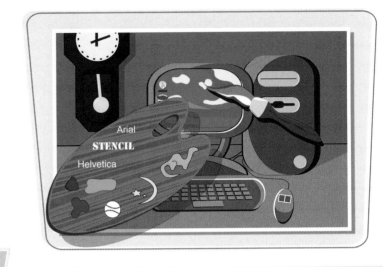

Change the Windows XP Colors and Fonts

1 Open the Display Properties dialog box.

Note: See the section "Open the Display Properties" earlier in this chapter.

2 Click the **Appearance** tab.

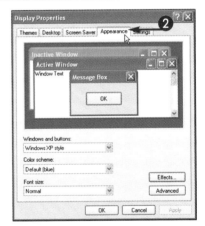

3 To choose an overall style, click ▾ in the **Windows and buttons** list and then click the style you want.

● These sample screen elements show the effect your changes will have.

4 Click ▾ in the **Color scheme** list, and then click the color scheme you want.

Note: The available color schemes depend on which style you selected in step 3.

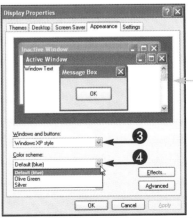

5 Click in the **Font Size** list, and then click the relative size you want.

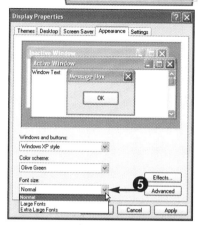

6 Click **OK** (or click **Apply** to leave the dialog box onscreen).

Windows XP applies the new colors and font size.

TIP

How can I improve the look of my on-screen text?

On most (but not all) screens, you can greatly improve the readability of text by activating Windows XP's ClearType feature:

1 In the Appearance tab, click **Effects**.

   The Effects dialog box appears.

2 Click in the list labeled "Use the following method to smooth edges of screen fonts," and then click **ClearType**.

3 Click **OK**.

4 Click in the Font size list and then click the relative size you want.

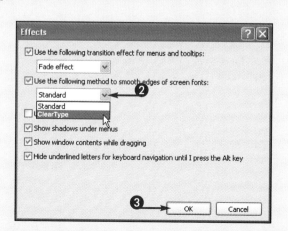

Rather than tweaking the background, screen saver, style, and colors individually, you can change all of these at once by applying a desktop theme.

Each desktop theme also includes its own set of desktop icons, mouse pointers, sound effects, fonts, and more.

Apply a Desktop Theme

① Open the Display Properties dialog box.

Note: See the section "Open the Display Properties" earlier in this chapter.

② Click the **Themes** tab.

③ Click ☑ in the **Theme** list, and then click the theme you want.

● The sample desktop shows what the theme will look like.

④ Click **OK** (or click **Apply** to leave the dialog box onscreen).

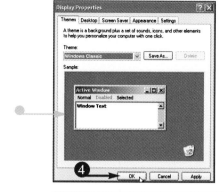

Windows XP applies the theme.

Note: *Many more Windows XP themes are available on the Internet. Run a search on "XP themes" in your favorite search engine and you will find many sites that enable you to download themes.*

TIP

Can I create my own theme?

Yes, by following these steps:

① Use the Display Properties dialog box to choose the theme elements, such as the desktop background, screen saver, style, colors, and font size.

② Click the **Themes** tab.

③ Click **Modified Theme** in the Theme list.

④ Click **Save As**.

⑤ Type a name for your theme.

⑥ Click **Save**.

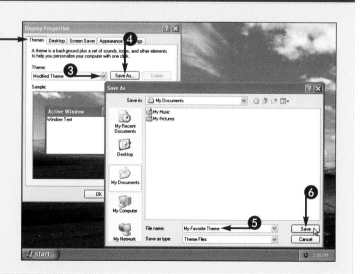

Change the Screen Resolution and Color Quality

You can select a higher screen resolution to see more information on your screen. You can also select a higher color quality to enhance your on-screen graphics.

The screen resolution is the number of pixels used in your screen display, and the color quality is the number of colors used in the display.

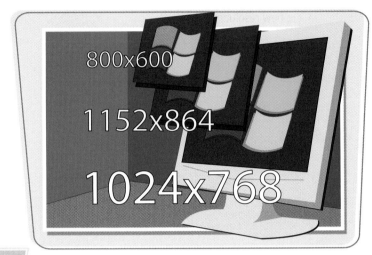

Change the Screen Resolution and Color Quality

① Open the Display Properties dialog box.

Note: *See the section "Open the Display Properties" earlier in this chapter.*

② Click the **Settings** tab.

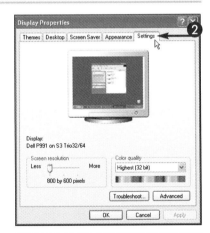

③ Drag the **Screen resolution** slider to the resolution you want.

Note: *Choosing a screen resolution that matches the size of the monitor you use is best. If you have a 14- or 15-inch monitor, use 800 x 600; for 17- or 19-inch monitors, use 1,024 x 768; for larger monitors, try 1,200 x 1,024 or even 1,600 x 1,200. Remember, however, that the larger the resolution, the smaller the screen images appear.*

● The sample screen shows you what your screen will look like at the new resolution.

④ Click ☑ in the **Color Quality** list, and then click the color quality you want.

Note: If you work with graphics regularly, choose the highest color-quality value.

⑤ Click **OK**.

The screen turns black and then returns with the new settings in effect.

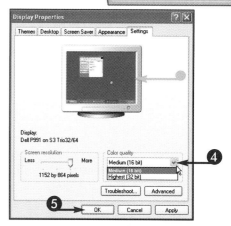

● In some cases, the Monitor Settings dialog box appears, asking if you want to keep the new settings.

⑥ Click **Yes**.

*Note: If changing the settings causes screen problems, click **No** to revert to your old settings. Alternatively, wait 15 seconds and Windows XP reverts to the old settings automatically.*

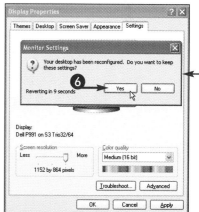

I have an old program that requires 640 x 480 resolution and 256 colors. How can I make the program run in Windows XP?

❶ Right-click the program's icon in the Start menu.

❷ Click **Properties**.

❸ Click the **Compatibility** tab.

❹ Click **Run in 256 colors** (☐ changes to ☑).

❺ Click **Run in 640 x 480 screen resolution** (☐ changes to ☑).

❻ Click **OK**.

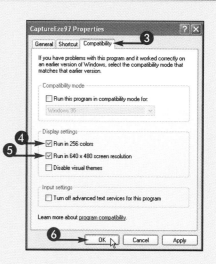

You can personalize how the Start menu looks and operates to suit your style and the way you work.

For example, you can switch to smaller icons to get more items on the menu, and you can show more of your most often used programs.

Customize the Start Menu

① Right-click **start**.

② Click **Properties**.

The Taskbar and Start Menu Properties dialog box appears.

③ Click the **Start Menu** tab.

④ Click **Start menu** (○ changes to ◉).

⑤ Click **Customize**.

The Customize Start Menu dialog box appears.

6 Click the **General** tab.

7 Click the icon size that you prefer (○ changes to ◉).

8 Change the maximum number of the most frequently used programs that can appear on the Start menu (type a number between 0 and 30; the default value is 6).

Note: To start over with a fresh list, click **Clear List**.

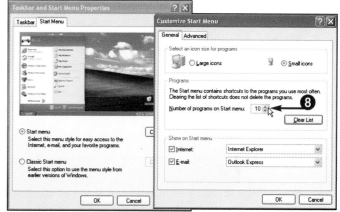

TIP

How do I remove a program that appears on my Start menu's list of most often used programs?

1 Click **start** to open the Start menu.

2 Right-click the program.

3 Click **Remove from This List**.

continued

To further personalize your
Start menu, you can change the
Internet and e-mail programs,
control the items that appear on
the right side of the menu, and
display a list of recently used
documents.

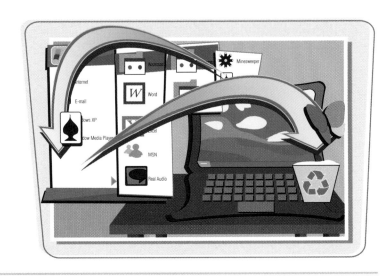

Customize the Start Menu *(continued)*

⑨ Click **Internet** to turn the Start menu's Internet icon
on (☐ changes to ☑) or off (☑ changes to ☐).

⑩ Click ☑, and click the Web browser you want to use
with the Start menu's Internet icon.

⑪ Click **E-mail** to turn the Start menu's E-mail icon on
(☐ changes to ☑) or off (☑ changes to ☐).

⑫ Click ☑, and click the e-mail program you want to
use with the Start menu's E-mail icon.

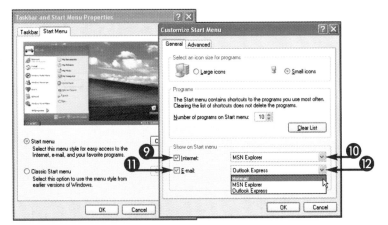

⑬ Click the **Advanced** tab.

⑭ Use the Start menu items list to control the icons
that appear on the right side of the Start menu.

Some items have several option buttons that control
how the item appears on the Start menu; click the
option you want (◯ changes to ◉).

Some items have check boxes that determine
whether the item appears or does not appear on the
Start menu.

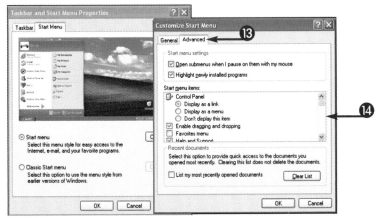

⑮ Click **List my most recently opened documents**
([ ] changes to [✓]) to add a menu of the last 15
documents you have used.

*Note: The menu appears as the My Recent Documents item on the right
side of the Start menu.*

*Note: To remove all the documents from this list, click **Clear List**.*

⑯ Click **OK**.

⑰ Click **OK**.

TIP

**How do I add a program permanently
to the Start menu?**

❶ Click **start** to open the Start menu.

❷ Right-click the program.

❸ Click **Pin to Start menu**.

The program now appears in the
top part of the menu, below the
Internet and E-mail icons.

You can personalize how the taskbar looks and operates to make it more efficient and to suit your own working style.

For example, you can unlock the taskbar for moving or resizing, temporarily hide the taskbar, and allow maximized windows to cover the taskbar.

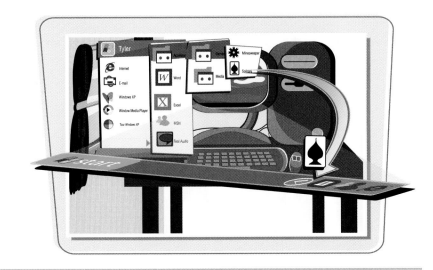

Customize the Taskbar

① Right-click an empty section of the taskbar.

② Click **Properties**.

The Taskbar and Start Menu Properties dialog box appears.

● These areas show you the effect that your changes will have on the taskbar.

③ Click **Lock the taskbar** (☑ changes to ☐) to unlock the taskbar so that you can resize or move it.

*Note: To quickly lock and unlock the taskbar, right-click an empty section of the taskbar and click **Lock the taskbar**.*

④ Click **Auto-hide the taskbar** (☐ changes to ☑) to hide the taskbar when you are using a program.

Note: To display the hidden taskbar, move your mouse pointer to the bottom edge of the screen.

⑤ Click **Keep the taskbar on top of other windows** (☑ changes to ☐) to allow maximized windows to use the full screen.

 TIPS

How do I resize the taskbar?

To resize the taskbar, click and drag the top edge of the taskbar up (to get more taskbar rows) or down (to get fewer taskbar rows).

How do I move the taskbar?

To move the taskbar, position the mouse ⌖ over an empty section of the taskbar, and then click and drag the taskbar to another edge of the screen.

continued

To further personalize your
Start menu, you can group
taskbar buttons, show the Quick
Launch toolbar, turn off the
clock, and reduce the number of
icons in the notification area.

Customize the Taskbar *(continued)*

6 Click **Group similar taskbar buttons** (☑ changes
to ☐) to disable the grouping of taskbar buttons.

7 Click **Show Quick Launch** (☐ changes to ☑) to
display the Quick Launch toolbar.

● Quick Launch gives you one-click access to several
Windows XP features.

● Starts Internet Explorer.

● Minimizes all open windows.

● Starts Windows Media Player.

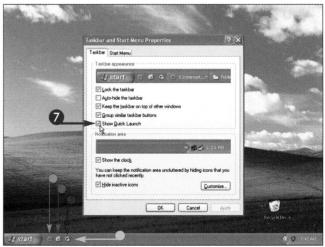

8 Click **Show the clock** (☑ changes to ☐) to hide the clock.

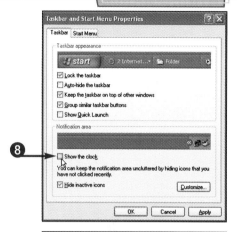

9 Click **Hide inactive icons** to display all the icons in the notification area.

Note: If you choose to leave the Hide inactive icons option on, you can click 🔽 to display the hidden icons. Click 🔽 again to hide the icons.

10 Click **OK**.

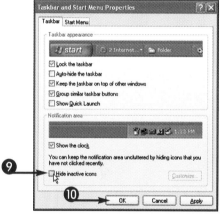

How do I use the Group Similar Taskbar Buttons feature?

Grouping taskbar buttons means showing only a single button for any program that has multiple windows open. To switch to one of those windows, click the taskbar button and then click the window name.

How can I control the display of notification area icons?

In the Taskbar and Start Menu Properties dialog box, click **Customize** to display the Customize Notifications dialog box. For each icon you want to work with, click 🔽, and then click the behavior you want: **Hide when inactive**, **Always hide**, or **Always show**.

Maintaining
Windows XP

To keep your system running smoothly, maintain top performance, and reduce the risk of computer problems, you need to perform some routine maintenance chores. This chapter shows you how to delete unnecessary files, check for hard drive errors, back up your files, and more.

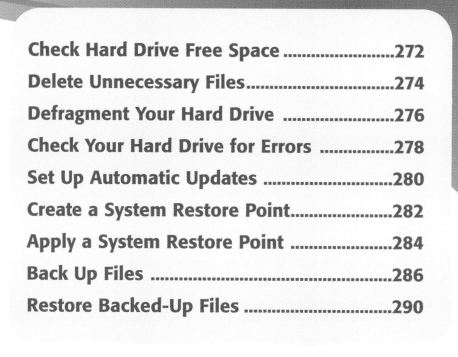

Check Hard Drive Free Space

If you run out of room on your hard drive, you will not be able to install more programs or create more documents. To ensure this does not happen, you can check how much free space your hard drive has.

Of particular concern is the hard drive on which Windows XP is installed, usually drive C. If this hard drive's free space gets low — say, less than 20 percent of the total hard drive space — Windows XP runs slower.

Check Hard Drive Free Space

① Click **start**.

② Click **My Computer**.

The My Computer window appears.

③ Click the drive you want to check.

Note: You can also check the free space on a CD-ROM, DVD-ROM, or floppy disk. Before you perform step 3, insert the disk in the drive.

④ Click in the **Details** area.

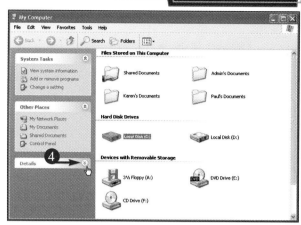

Information about the disk appears.

● This area displays the amount of free space on the drive.

● This area displays the total amount of space on the drive.

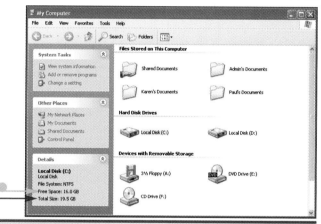

TIPS

How often should I check my hard drive free space?

With normal computer use, you should check your hard drive free space about once a month. If you install programs, create large files, or download media frequently, you should probably check your free space every couple of weeks.

What can I do if my hard drive space is getting low?

You can do three things:

Delete Documents

If you have documents — particularly media files such as images, music, and videos — that you are sure you no longer need, delete them.

Remove Programs

If you have programs that you no longer use, uninstall them.

For more on uninstalling programs, see Chapter 2.

Run Disk Cleanup

Use the Disk Cleanup program to delete files that Windows XP no longer uses. See the next section "Delete Unnecessary Files."

Delete Unnecessary Files

To free up hard drive space on your computer and keep Windows XP running efficiently, you can use the Disk Cleanup program to delete files that your system no longer needs.

Run Disk Cleanup any time that your hard drive free space gets too low. If hard drive space is not a problem, run Disk Cleanup every two or three months.

Delete Unnecessary Files

1 Click **start**.

2 Click **All Programs**.

3 Click **Accessories**.

4 Click **System Tools**.

5 Click **Disk Cleanup**.

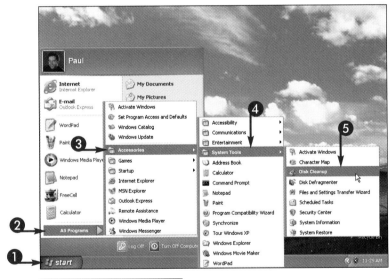

If your computer has more than one drive, the Select Drive dialog box appears.

6 Click the ☑ in the **Drives** list and then click the hard drive you want to clean up.

7 Click **OK**.

The Disk Cleanup dialog box appears.

- This area displays the total amount of drive space you can free up.

- This area displays the amount of drive space the activated options will free up.

8 Click the check box (☐ changes to ☑) for each file type that you want to delete.

- This area displays a description of the highlighted file type.

9 Click **OK**.

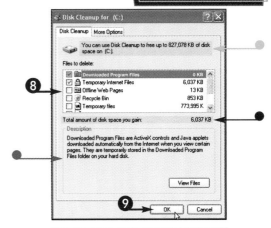

- Disk Cleanup asks you to confirm that you want to delete the file types.

10 Click **Yes**.

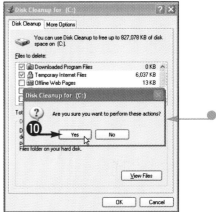

TIP

What types of files does Disk Cleanup delete?

Downloaded Program Files	Small Web page programs that are downloaded onto your hard drive.
Temporary Internet files	Web page copies stored on your hard drive for faster viewing.
Offline Web pages	Web page copies stored on your hard drive for offline viewing.
Recycle Bin	Files that you have deleted recently.
Temporary files	Files used by programs to store temporary data.
WebClient/Publisher temporary files	Copies of files used to improve the performance of the WebClient/Publisher service.
Catalog files for the Content Indexer	Old files that were once used to speed up file searches.

Defragment Your Hard Drive

You can make Windows XP and your programs run faster, and your documents open quicker, by defragmenting your hard drive.

Most files are stored on your computer in several pieces, and over time those pieces often get scattered around your hard drive. Defragmenting improves performance by bringing all those pieces together, which makes finding and opening each file faster.

Defragment Your Hard Drive

1 Click **start**.

2 Click **All Programs**.

3 Click **Accessories**.

4 Click **System Tools**.

5 Click **Disk Defragmenter**.

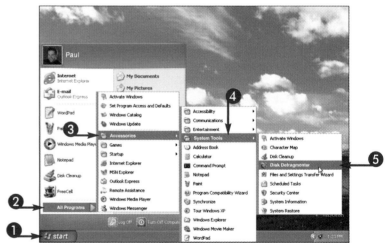

The Disk Defragmenter window appears.

6 Click the hard drive that you want to work with.

7 Click **Analyze**.

Disk Defragmenter checks the hard drive to see if you need to defragment it.

Disk Defragmenter displays a summary dialog box when it completes the analysis.

8 Click **Defragment** if you want to defragment your hard drive.

● Click **Close** if you do not want to defragment your hard drive.

● A dialog box appears when the defragmentation is complete.

9 Click **Close**.

10 Click Close (⊠) to close Disk Defragmenter.

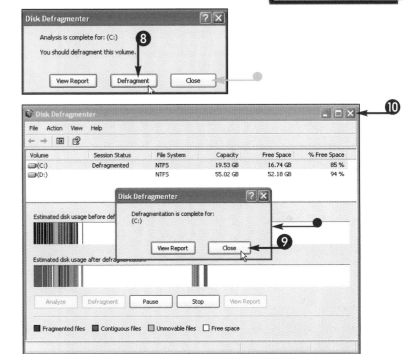

How often should I defragment my hard drive?

This depends on how often you use your computer. If you use your computer every day, you should defragment your hard drive once a week. If you use your computer only occasionally, you should defragment your hard drive every two or three months.

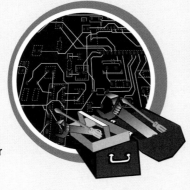

How long will defragmenting my hard drive take?

It depends on the size of the hard drive, the amount of data on it, and the extent of the defragmentation. Budget at least 15 minutes for the defragment, and know that it could take over an hour.

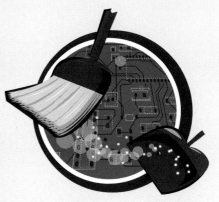

Check Your Hard Drive for Errors

Because hard drive errors can cause files to become corrupted, which may prevent you from running a program or opening a document, you can use the Check Disk program to look for and fix hard drive errors.

① Click **start**.

② Click **My Computer**.

The My Computer window appears.

③ Click the hard drive that you want to check.

④ Click **File**.

⑤ Click **Properties**.

The hard drive's Properties dialog box appears.

⑥ Click the **Tools** tab.

⑦ Click **Check Now**.

The Check Disk dialog box appears.

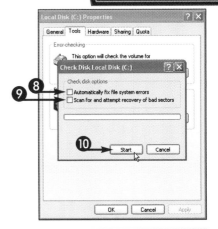

8 If you want Check Disk to fix any errors it finds, click **Automatically fix file system errors** (☐ changes to ☑).

9 If you want Check Disk to look for bad sectors, check **Scan for and attempt recovery of bad sectors** (☐ changes to ☑).

10 Click **Start**.

The Hard drive check begins.

If Check Disk finds any errors and you did not click the **Automatically fix file system errors** option, follow the instructions provided by the program.

● A dialog box appears when the drive check is over.

11 Click **OK** to return to the hard drive's Properties dialog box.

12 Click **OK**.

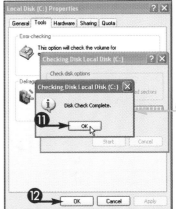

 TIPS

What is a "bad sector"?

A *sector* is a small storage location on your hard drive. When Windows XP saves a file on the drive, it divides the file into pieces and stores each piece in a separate sector. A bad sector is one that, through physical damage or some other cause, can no longer be used to reliably store data.

How often should I check for hard drive errors?

You should perform the basic hard drive check about once a week. Perform the more thorough bad sector check once a month. Note that the bad sector check can take several hours, depending on the size of the drive, so only perform this check when you will not be needing your computer for a while.

Set Up Automatic Updates

Microsoft makes Windows XP updates available from time to time. These updates fix problems and resolve security issues. You can reduce computer problems and maximize online safety by setting up Windows XP to download and install these updates automatically.

You must be logged on to Windows XP with an Administrator account to set up automatic updates. See Chapter 7, "Sharing Your Computer with Others."

Set Up Automatic Updates

❶ Click the Windows Security Alerts icon in the taskbar's notification area.

*Note: If you do not see the Windows Security Alerts icon, click **start**, click **All Programs**, click **Accessories**, click **System Tools**, and then click **Security Center**.*

The Security Center window appears.

❷ Click **System**.

The System Properties dialog box appears.

3 Click the **Automatic Updates** tab.

4 Click **Automatic** (◯ changes to ◉).

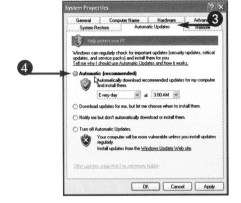

5 Click ▾, and then click the day when you want the automatic updates to occur.

6 Click ▾, and then click the time of day when you want the automatic updates to occur.

7 Click **OK**.

8 Click ☒ to close the Security Center window.

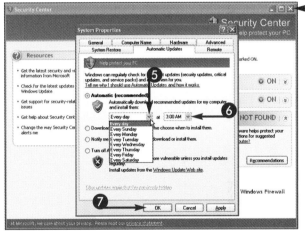

TIP

How do I set up automatic updates if I do not have Service Pack 2?

1 Click **start**.

2 Right-click **My Computer**.

3 Click **Properties**.

The System Properties dialog box appears.

4 Click the **Automatic Updates** tab.

5 Click this option (◯ changes to ◉).

6 Click **OK**.

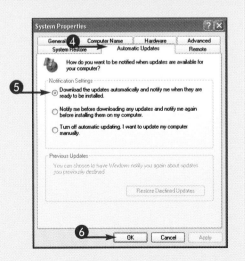

Create a System Restore Point

If your computer crashes or becomes unstable after installing a program or a new device, Windows XP's System Restore feature can fix things by restoring the system to its previous state. To ensure this works, you need to set restore points when you install things on your computer.

Windows XP automatically creates system restore points as follows: every 24 hours (called a *system checkpoint*), before installing an update, and before installing certain programs (such as Microsoft Office) and devices.

Create a System Restore Point

① Click **start**.

② Click **All Programs**.

③ Click **Accessories**.

④ Click **System Tools**.

⑤ Click **System Restore**.

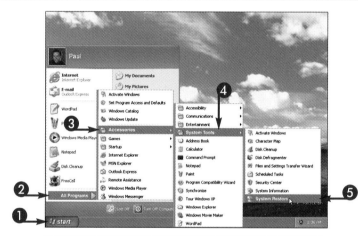

The System Restore window appears.

⑥ Click **Create a restore point** (○ changes to ◉).

⑦ Click **Next**.

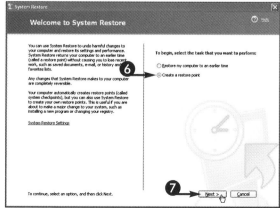

The Create a Restore Point window appears.

8 Type a description for your restore point.

9 Click **Create**.

System Restore creates the restore point.

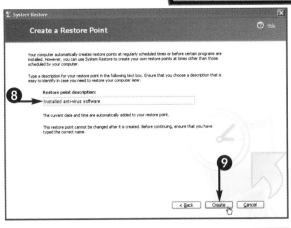

The Restore Point Created window appears.

10 Click **Close**.

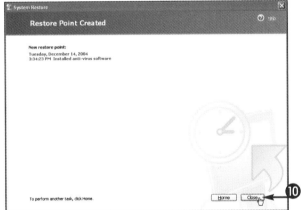

When should I create a restore point?

To be safe, you should create a restore point before you install any software, whether you purchased the program at a store or downloaded it from the Internet. You should also create a restore point before you add any new hardware devices to your system.

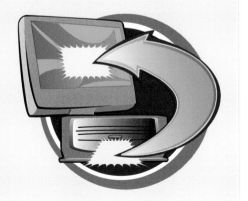

Apply a System Restore Point

If your computer becomes unstable or behaves erratically after installing a program or device, you can often fix the problem by applying the restore point you created before making the change.

When you apply a restore point, Windows XP reverts your computer to the configuration it had when you created the restore point.

Apply a System Restore Point

① Save all your open documents and close all your open programs.

② Click **start**.

③ Click **All Programs**.

④ Click **Accessories**.

⑤ Click **System Tools**.

⑥ Click **System Restore**.

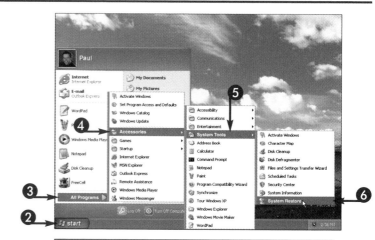

The System Restore window appears.

⑦ Click **Restore my computer to an earlier time** (○ changes to ⊙).

⑧ Click **Next**.

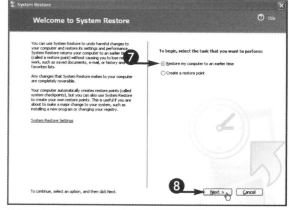

The Select a Restore Point window appears.

9 Click the date that contains the restore point.

10 Click the restore point you want to apply.

11 Click **Next**.

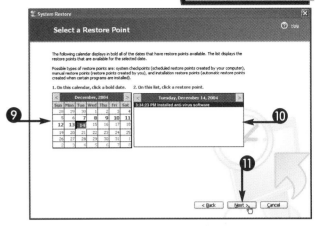

The Confirm Restore Point Selection window appears.

12 Confirm that this is the correct restore point.

*Note: If the restore point is incorrect, click **Back** to choose the correct restore point.*

13 Click **Next**.

System Restore applies the restore point and then restarts Windows XP.

When Windows XP restarts, the Restoration Complete window appears.

14 Click **OK**.

TIPS

Will I lose any of my recent work when I apply a restore point?

No, the restore point only reverts your computer's configuration back to the earlier time. Any work you performed in the interim — documents you created, e-mails you received, Web page favorites you saved, and so on — is not affected by applying the restore point.

If applying the restore point makes things worse, can I reverse it?

Yes. Follow steps **1** to **6** to open the System Restore window. Click **Undo my last restoration** (○ changes to ◉), and then follow steps **8** to **14**.

You can use the Backup program to make backup copies of your important files. If a system problem causes you to lose one or more files, you can restore them from the backup.

Back Up Files

① Click **start**.

② Click **All Programs**.

③ Click **Accessories**.

④ Click **System Tools**.

⑤ Click **Backup**.

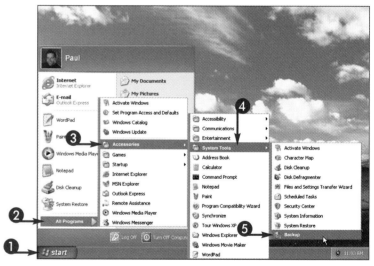

The Backup or Restore Wizard appears.

⑥ Click **Next**.

The Backup or Restore dialog box appears.

⑦ Click **Back up files and settings** (○ changes to ⊙).

⑧ Click **Next**.

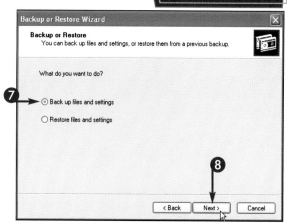

The What to Back Up dialog box appears.

⑨ Click **My documents and settings** (○ changes to ⊙).

⑩ Click **Next**.

The Backup Type, Destination, and Name dialog box appears.

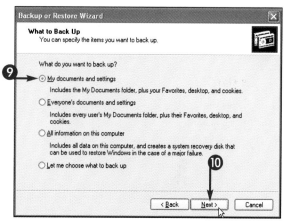

TIP

How do I install Backup if I have Windows XP Home Edition?

❶ Insert your Windows XP Home Edition CD.

Note: If you see the Welcome to Microsoft Windows XP screen after a few seconds, click Exit to close it.

❷ Click **start**.

❸ Click **My Computer**.

❹ Right-click the icon for your CD-ROM drive.

❺ Click **Open**.

❻ Double-click the **VALUEADD** folder.

❼ Double-click the **MSFT** folder.

❽ Double-click the **NTBACKUP** folder.

❾ Double-click the **NTBACKUP** file.

❿ Click **Finish**.

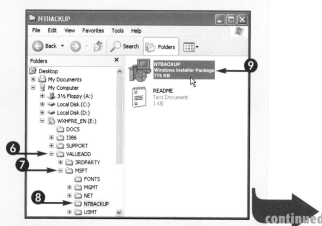

continued

Rather than using floppy disks, which hold only a small amount of data, you can save time by backing up to a storage medium that has a greater capacity.

You can back up to a Zip disk, a second internal hard drive, an external hard drive, a flash drive, a network folder, and a tape drive.

Back Up Files *(continued)*

⑪ Click 🔽 to choose the backup type.

*Note: The **Select the backup type** list is only available if you have a tape drive on your system.*

⑫ Click 🔽 to choose the location for the backup file.

*Note: To choose a location other than a floppy disk, click **Browse**.*

⑬ Type a name for the backup.

⑭ Click **Next**.

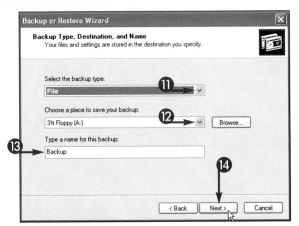

The Completing the Backup or Restore Wizard dialog box appears.

⑮ Click **Finish**.

The Backup Progress dialog box appears while the program backs up your documents and settings.

● If the medium to which you are backing up becomes full, the Insert Media dialog box appears.

⑯ Remove the full medium and replace it with a new one.

Note: *If your backup requires multiple media, you should give each medium a label, such as Backup 1, Backup 2, and so on.*

⑰ Click **OK**.

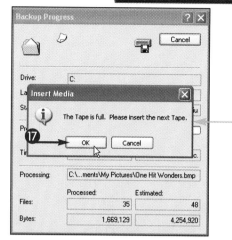

⑱ When the backup is complete, click **Close**.

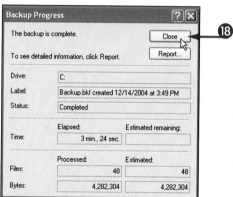

 TIPS

Can I back up to a recordable CD?

The Backup program does not allow you to choose a recordable CD as the backup location. To work around this limitation, select a location on your hard drive for the backup file. When the backup is complete, copy the backup file to the CD; see "Copy Files to a CD" in Chapter 7. Note, however, that the resulting backup file must be no more than 650MB to fit on the CD. See the next tip to learn how to back up only certain files.

Can I back up only certain files?

Yes. Follow steps **1** to **8** in the **Back Up Files** task to display the What to Back Up dialog box. Click **"Let me choose what to back up"** (○ changes to ⦿) and click **Next**. In the Items to Back Up dialog box, follow these steps:

❶ Click the check boxes of the files you want to include in the backup (☐ changes to ☑).

❷ Click **Next**.

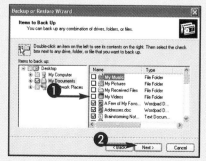

Restore Backed-Up Files

You can restore a file from a backup if the file is lost because of a system problem or because you accidentally deleted or overwrote the file.

Restore Backed-Up Files

① Click **start**.

② Click **All Programs**.

③ Click **Accessories**.

④ Click **System Tools**.

⑤ Click **Backup**.

The Backup or Restore Wizard appears.

⑥ Click **Next**.

The Backup or Restore dialog box appears.

7 Click **Restore files and settings** (○ changes to ⊙).

8 Click **Next**.

The What to Restore dialog box appears.

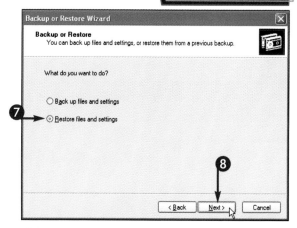

9 Click ⊞ to expand the File branch (⊞ changes to ⊟).

10 Click ⊞ to expand the branch of the backup file from which you want to restore the files (⊞ changes to ⊟).

11 Click ⊞ on each folder you need to open to get to the folder that contains the files you want to restore (⊞ changes to ⊟).

12 Click the folder that contains the files you want to restore.

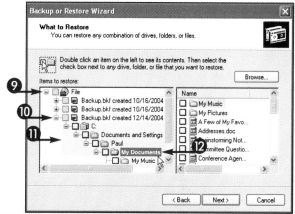

 TIP

Can I delete some of the backup files that appear in the What to Restore list?

Yes, you can. This is a good idea because having fewer backup files to deal with makes it much easier to find the one you want. And since the backup files are dated, it is easy just to delete the older backups that you no longer need. Follow these steps to delete a backup file:

1 Right-click the backup file that you want to delete.

2 Click **Delete catalog**.

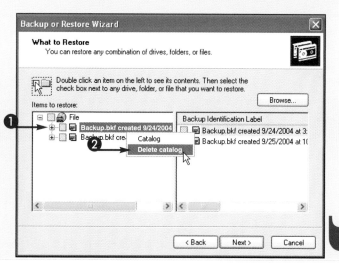

continued

You can restore all of the backed-up files, or you can restore just one or more of the backed-up files.

Restore Backed-Up Files *(continued)*

⑬ Click the check boxes of the files you want to restore (☐ changes to ☑).

⑭ Click **Next**.

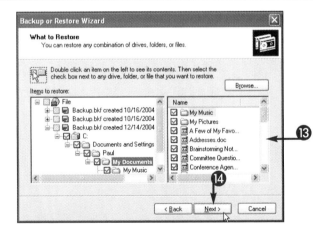

The Completing the Backup or Restore Wizard dialog box appears.

⑮ Insert the medium that contains the backup file.

⑯ Click **Finish**.

The Restore Progress dialog box appears while the program restores your files.

● If Backup requires another medium, the Insert Media dialog box appears.

⑰ Remove the current medium and replace it with the required one.

⑱ Click **OK**.

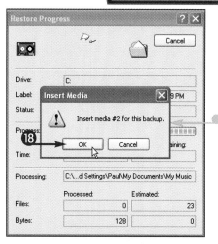

⑲ When the restore is complete, click **Close**.

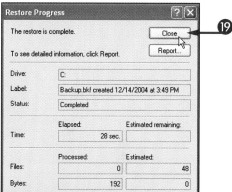

TIP

If I want to restore all the files in a backup that appears in the What to Restore list, do I have to select them all individually?

No. Here is a quick method for selecting all the backed-up files in the What to Restore dialog box:

❶ Click ⊞ to expand the File branch (⊞ changes to ⊟).

❷ Click ⊞ to expand the branch of the backup file from which you want to restore the files (⊞ changes to ⊟).

❸ Click the check boxes of the drives that appear (☐ changes to ☑).

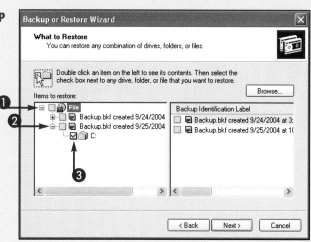

Networking with Windows XP

A network is a collection of computers that are connected using either cables or a wireless hookup. Assuming you already have your computers connected, this chapter shows you how to work with the other computers on your network, and how to share your computer's resources with other network users.

View Network Resources

To see what other network users have shared on the network, you can use the My Network Places folder to view the other computers and see their shared resources.

A network resource can be a folder, hard drive, CD or DVD drive, removable disk drive, printer, scanner, or other shared device.

① Click **start**.

② Click **My Network Places**.

The My Network Places window appears.

● Some of the network resources appear in this area.

③ Click **View Workgroup Computers**.

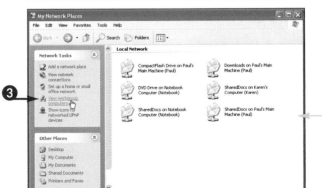

The computers in your network workgroup appear.

● The name of the workgroup appears here.

● The computers in the workgroup appear here.

④ Double-click the icon of the computer you want to work with.

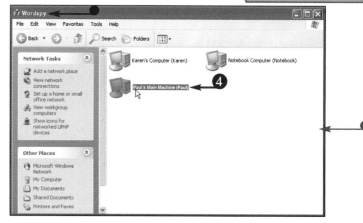

● The computer's shared network resources appear.

Note: *If you have a folder you want to share with the network, see the section "Share a Folder," later in this chapter.*

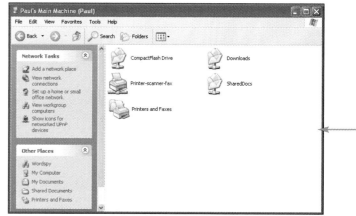

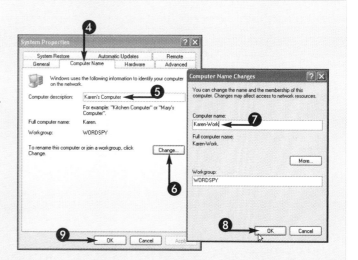

TIP

How do I change the network name and description of my computer?

① Click **start**.

② Right-click **My Computer**.

③ Click **Properties**.

④ Click the **Computer Name** tab.

⑤ Type the new computer description here.

⑥ Click **Change**.

⑦ Type the new computer name here.

⑧ Click **OK**.

⑨ Click **OK**.

⑩ Restart your computer.

Set Up a
Network Place

If a shared network folder or drive does not appear in your My Network Places folder, you can access the resource easier if you set it up as a network place.

① Click **start**.

② Click **My Network Places**.

The My Network Places window appears.

③ Click **Add a network place**.

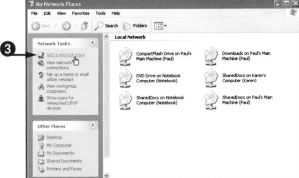

The Add Network Place Wizard appears.

④ Click **Next**.

⑤ If the Dial-Up Connection dialog box appears, click **Cancel**.

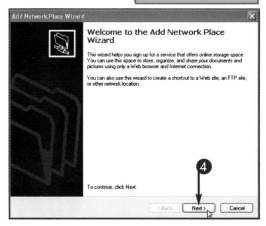

⑥ Click **Choose another network location**.

⑦ Click **Next**.

The dialog box asking for the address of the network place appears.

Can I remove icons from the My Network Places folder?

Yes. Click the icon you want to remove and then press `Delete`. Windows XP asks you to confirm the deletion. Click **Yes**.

Is it possible to arrange the My Network Places icons by computer?

① Click **View**.

② Click **Arrange Icons by**.

③ Click **Computer**.

Windows XP arranges the icons in groups for each computer.

continued

You can only set up shared folders and disk drives as network places. You cannot set up shared devices such as printers and scanners as network places.

Set Up a Network Place *(continued)*

8 Click **Browse**.

9 Click ⊞ to open the Entire Network branch (⊞ changes to ⊟).

10 Click ⊞ to open the Microsoft Windows Network branch (⊞ changes to ⊟).

11 Click ⊞ to open your workgroup branch (⊞ changes to ⊟).

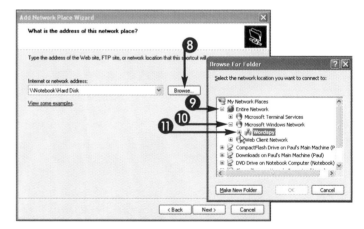

12 Click ⊞ to open the workgroup computer branch (⊞ changes to ⊟).

13 Click the shared resource you want to set up as a network place.

14 Click **OK**.

15 Click **Next**.

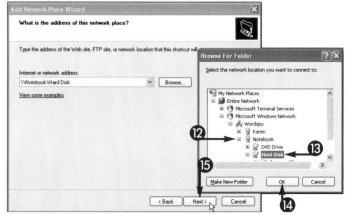

A dialog box asking you to name the network place appears.

⑯ Type a name for the network place.

⑰ Click **Next**.

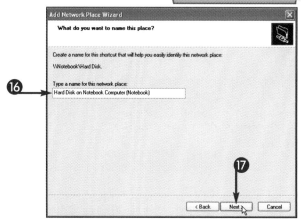

The Completing the Add Network Place Wizard dialog box appears.

⑱ If you do not want to view the contents of the network place, click **Open this network place when I click Finish** (☑ changes to ☐).

⑲ Click **Finish**.

The new network place appears in the My Network Places folder.

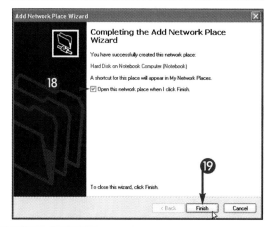

TIPS

When another user is working with a file from a network place, what happens if I try to use the same file?

It depends on the program you are using. Some programs do not let you open the file at all. In other cases, the program allows you to view but not make changes to the file. More rarely, a few programs — particularly databases — allow both people to use the same file.

Why do I sometimes get a "network path was not found" error message when I double-click a network place to open it?

This usually happens when the computer sharing the network place is turned off or no longer connected to the network. It may also mean that the other computer is no longer sharing the resource.

Turn a Network Folder into a Disk Drive

You can set up a connection to a shared network folder that makes the folder appear as though it is a disk drive on your computer. This gives you even easier access to the network folder via the My Computer window.

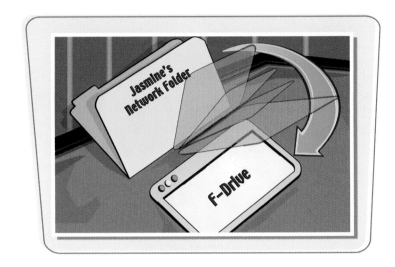

Turn a Network Folder into a Disk Drive

① Click **start**.

② Click **My Network Places**.

The My Network Places window appears.

③ Click **Tools**.

④ Click **Map Network Drive**.

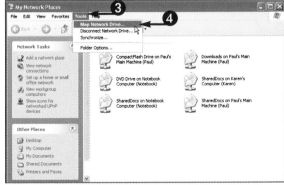

The Map Network Drive dialog box appears.

5 Click **Browse**.

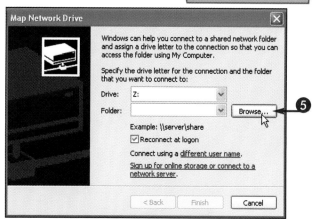

The Browse For Folder dialog box appears.

6 Click the shared network folder you want to work with.

7 Click **OK** to return to the Map Network Drive dialog box.

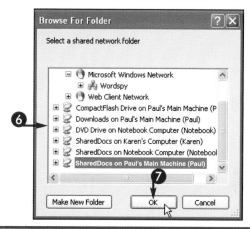

Does the network folder become an actual disk drive on my computer?

No. The folder remains on the network, but Windows XP *maps* the folder to appear as though it is a disk drive on your computer.

I have a program that does not work with network folders. How can I fix this?

Some software is programmed to work only with local files and cannot handle network folders directly. You can work around this problem by turning the network folder into a disk drive that appears to be part of your local computer.

continued

You assign one of your computer's available disk drive letters to the network folder, and that letter becomes part of the disk drive collection on your computer.

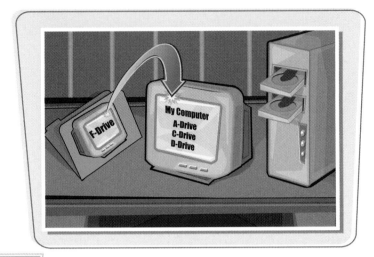

Turn a Network Folder into a Disk Drive *(continued)*

8 Click ▼ in the **Drive** list, and then click the drive letter you want to assign to the network folder.

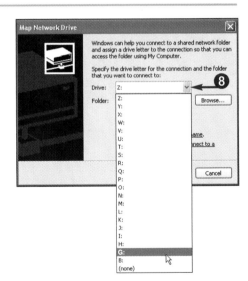

9 If you do not want Windows XP to assign the drive letter to the network folder each time you start your computer, click **Reconnect at logon** (☑ changes to ☐).

10 Click **Finish**.

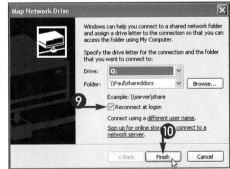

- A window showing the contents of the network folder appears.

⑪ Click **My Computer**.

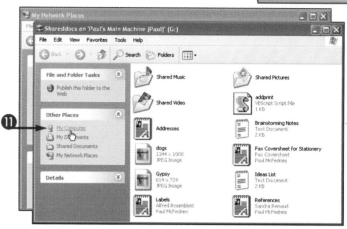

The My Computer window appears.

- An icon for the drive letter appears in My Computer's Network Drives section.

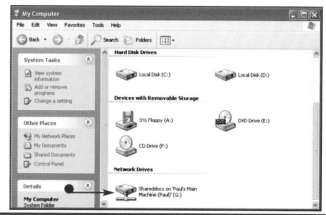

Is there a limit to the number of network folders I can turn into disk drives?

Yes, but you are only limited by the number of available drive letters on your computer. For example, suppose your computer has a floppy disk drive (drive A), two hard disk drives (drives C and D), a CD-ROM drive (drive E), and a DVD-ROM drive (drive F). This leaves 21 available drive letters: B and G through Z.

How do I disconnect a drive letter assigned to a network folder?

① Open the My Network Places window.

② Click **My Computer**.

③ In the Network Drives section, right-click the network drive you want to disconnect.

④ Click **Disconnect**.

Print over the Network

You can send a document from your computer to a shared printer attached to a network computer. This enables you to use just a single printer for all the computers in your network.

Print over the Network

CONNECT TO A NETWORK PRINTER

1 Use My Network Places to open the network computer that shares the printer you want to use.

Note: *See "View Network Resources" earlier in this chapter.*

2 Click the shared printer.

3 Click **File**.

4 Click **Connect**.

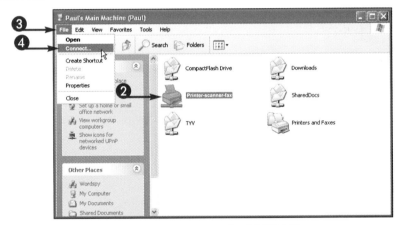

A warning dialog box appears.

5 Click **Yes**.

Windows XP installs the printer on your computer.

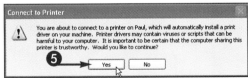

PRINT USING THE NETWORK PRINTER

1 Open the document you want to print.

2 Click **File**.

3 Click **Print**.

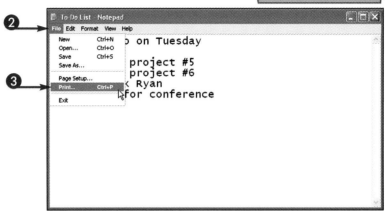

The Print dialog box appears.

4 Click the network printer.

5 Click **Print**.

The document prints on the network printer.

Note: If you have a printer you want to share with the network, see the section "Share a Printer" later in this chapter.

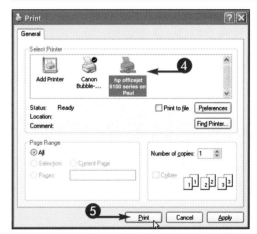

How do I make the network printer my default printer?

1 Click **start**.

2 Click **Control Panel**.

3 Click **Printers and Other Hardware**.

4 Click **View installed printers or fax printers**.

5 Click the network printer.

6 Click **File**.

7 Click **Set as Default Printer**.

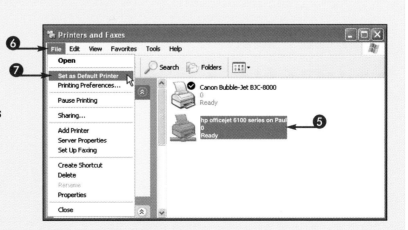

Share a Folder

You can share one of your folders on the network, enabling other network users to view and optionally edit the files you place in that folder.

Sharing a folder enables you to work on a file with other people without having to send them a copy of the file.

① Click the folder that you want to share.

② Click **Share this folder**.

The folder's Properties dialog box appears.

③ Click **Share this folder on the network** (☐ changes to ☑).

Note: *The folder's share name, which you can edit in this tab, is the name that network users see when they view your computer's resources. Changing this name does not change the folder's actual name.*

④ If you want to enable the network users to make changes to the shared files, click **Allow network users to change my files** (☐ changes to ☑).

⑤ Click **OK**.

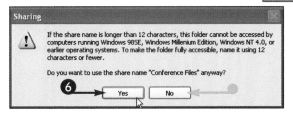

If the share name is longer than 12 characters, a dialog box appears to warn you that older computers may not be able to access the folder.

⑥ To continue with the existing name, click **Yes**.

● If you know that other network users have computers running older versions of Windows, click **No**, and edit the name to 12 characters or less, and go back to step **6**.

● Windows XP adds a hand () under the folder's icon to indicate that the folder is shared on the network.

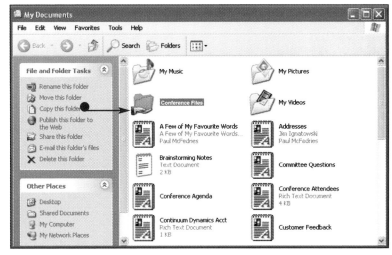

TIPS

Is there an easier way to share files on the network?

Yes. Click **start**, and then click **My Computer** to open the My Computer window. In the Files Stored on This Computer section, you will see a folder named Shared Documents, which is automatically shared on the network. Any files you add to this folder are available for viewing or editing by other network users.

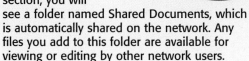

How do I stop sharing a folder?

① Click the folder you want to stop sharing.

② Click Share this folder.

The folder's Properties dialog box appears.

③ Click **Share this folder on the network** (☑ changes to ☐).

④ Click **OK**.

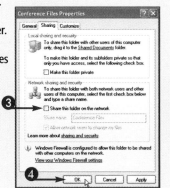

Share a Printer

If you have a printer connected to your computer, you can share the printer with the network, enabling other network users to send their documents to your printer.

Sharing a printer saves money and time because you only have to purchase and configure one printer for all the computers on your network.

① Click **start**.

② Click **Control Panel**.

The Control Panel window appears.

③ Click **Printers and Other Hardware**.

The Printers and Other Hardware window appears.

④ Click **View installed printers or fax printers**.

The Printers and Faxes window appears.

⑤ Click the printer you want to share.

⑥ Click **Share this printer**.

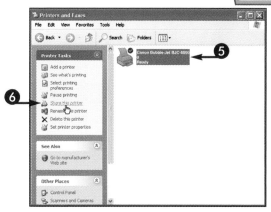

● The printer's Properties dialog box appears.

⑦ Click **Share this printer** (○ changes to ◉).

⑧ Edit the share name of the printer if you want to change it.

⑨ Click **OK**.

● Windows XP adds a 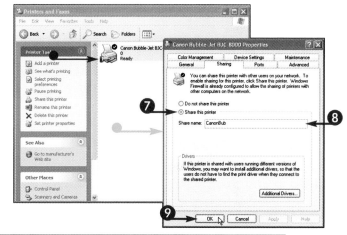 under the printer's icon to indicate that the printer is shared on the network.

TIP

Will users of other Windows versions be able to use the shared printer?

Yes, but you can make those users' lives easier by installing the printer files that are required by the other Windows versions:

① Repeat steps **1** to **6** of this task to open the printer's Properties dialog box.

② Click **Additional Drivers**.

The Additional Drivers dialog box opens.

③ For each version of Windows used on your network, click the check box (☐ changes to ☑).

④ Click **OK** to close the Additional Drivers dialog box.

⑤ Click **OK** to close the printer's Properties dialog box.

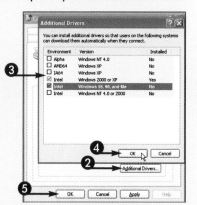

Index

Index

Index

Index